COMING ALIVE
with
RAYCHEL

BY RAYCHEL

and

BY MARK SOLOMON, Ph.D.

The information presented and opinions expressed in this book are based upon the research, experience and observations of Raychel. It is not her intention to diagnose, prescribe, or in any way take the place of qualified health professionals.

If you have any question as to the appropriateness of any of the suggestions, opinions, or information contained in this book, consult your physician or other qualified health professional.

If you use this information without your doctor's approval the authors and publisher assume no responsibility.

Dedicated

to

THE UNIVERSAL

SOURCE

That Inspired

Guided and

Orchestrated

the events

that made

this book

HAPPEN

R. S.

CONTENTS

PREFACE

On a clear, warm, January day in 1986 there was excitement at the Institute. The Santa Ana conditions had brought the temperatures into the mid-80's and the guests knew that they had surely been blessed. Some had come from very cold climates to the north, and saw this weather as a good sign. The gentle breeze that blew over the grounds added to the anticipation, for the guests knew that with a wind the helium-filled balloons would ascend rapidly, carrying away their worst fears and apprehensions.

There was laughter and talk and writing. Each guest would write a single word or phrase on a slip of paper. The message contained the trait or condition or fear that she or he most wanted to let go of. For some it was weight, extra pounds. For some it was cancer. For others it was a habit or attitude that no longer served a seemingly useful purpose.

When each guest had tied the message to the string that was attached to his or her balloon, a circle formed. As I looked around the circle of guests, I saw not a collection of unhealthy people, but a gathering of lovely and loving souls, each with a determination to be the best human being possible.

Slowly I counted, "One. . .two. . .three," then, "Let go and let God!" With that, scores of colored balloons ascended to the heavens and with them went as many anxieties and fears. This was a symbolic act, repeated each

Monday at the Institute, an act which carries with it great hope and promise. Guests could feel the burdens being lifted from them, for they knew that their energies had been released and they were coming alive!

As I watched the balloons rising, I thought about the program and the many thousands who have benefitted from it over the past ten years. People have come from throughout the world — Europe, Great Britain, Scandinavia, South America, China, Mexico, Japan, Australia, the fifty States, Canada, Asia, and elsewhere. There have been people from all walks of life, from those of modest means to the wealthy, from the dispossessed to the socially prominent. There have been couples with infant children, youngsters as young as two and youngsters as old as ninety-two.

The reasons that these people have come to the Optimum Health Institute of San Diego are varied. Some have come to shed unwanted pounds. Others have been told that they have cancer and that their time is short. Others have had diabetes or other dis-eases of nutritional imbalance, while still others simply have wanted to cleanse themselves of toxins built up over many years or unwind from the stresses of their day-to-day lives.

Some people have come as skeptics and have left feeling healthier and more positive about themselves. Nearly one-third of each week's class has been composed of those who have been through the program before. Some, in fact, are regulars, who come here periodically to detoxify and to share in the love and positive atmosphere which pervades our Institute.

But regardless of the reasons that have brought people here over the past ten years, one thing is clear: The changes I see in people are dramatic and positive. The focus here is not on sickness. The emphasis is on health. We cannot offer cures, because it is our belief, based on experience and observation, that the body, given the proper tools, heals itself. What we teach is a balanced program which encourages optimum physical, mental, emotional, and spiritual health.

It is my belief that in order to be whole, a person cannot neglect any part of the being. What we eat, what we think, what we feel, and how we see ourselves in relation to the universe, are all essential ingredients in optimum health. What I have learned over the past thirty-five years of active searching, and the results I have seen in the past decade as the director of the Institute, have reinforced that belief.

Come with me now, if you will. Join me as I take a journey with a new friend, a friend who is a composite of the many thousands of friends who have been to the Institute. Listen as we chat. Watch as I share with him many wonderful techniques for achieving optimum health. Join in, if you like.

OH, HERE HE COMES NOW. . .

INTRODUCTION

Hi, kiddo. How do you feel?

Well, Raychel, to tell you the truth, I feel...
...okay.
...not bad.
...I've felt better.
...kind of run down.
...fat.
...lonely and depressed.
...so-so.
...pretty well, considering.
...ugly.
...sluggish.
...stopped up.
. . .
. . .

How would you like to feel?

Naturally, I'd like to feel. . .
  . . .terrific!
  . . .wonderful!
  . . .on top of the world!
  . . .better and better!
  . . .healthier and healthier!
  . . .happier and happier all the time!
  . . .alive and feeling great!
  . . .
  . . .

Now, that's better! I like exclamation points! In fact, I love exclamation points! I'll take two!!

I want to talk about terrific! Let's talk about coming alive!! Let's maximize the quality of your life. How about achieving optimum health, balanced health?

Yeah, but. . .
  . . .I'm too old.
  . . .I don't feel that bad.
  . . .I have others to think about. I'll look after
    myself later.
  . . .I've always been overweight.
  . . .I have big bones.
  . . .poor health runs in my family.
  . . .I've adjusted.
  . . .
  . . .

I bet you think I'm going to argue with you. Well, I'm not. If you want to feel lousy or just okay, go ahead. Not me, boy!

Yeah, but...
...I can't help it.
...she made me feel that way.
...it's too late.
...there's no hope.
...I can get by.
...things could be worse.
...that's just the way I am.
. . .
. . .

Excuses! Excuses! Yeabuts! Yeabuts! I've heard so many over the years. But maybe I haven't heard them all. Go on.

Now you're getting me mad!

Great! An exclamation point! Now we're on the right track. You're terrrrrrrific!

Look, only you are responsible for your own health and for the quality of your life. Your mother isn't. Your children aren't. Your grocer isn't. Your banker isn't. I'm not.

I am responsible for my own health and happiness, and let me tell you, when I learned that, I was on my way to achieving optimum health. I began to come alive!

Boy, I wish I had your enthusiasm.

So you want my enthusiasm. Well, you can't have it. But you can certainly have your own. We can both be enthusiastic. You win! I win! We win!

Let's start with a short health quiz, just a few questions...

CHAPTER ONE

Balanced Health

How's your health? Is it balanced?

Gee, I don't know. I eat too much sugar and drink a little more coffee than I should. But I eat lots of vegetables and salads and I drink milk for calcium. I eat meat for protein, though I've cut down lately. Some people are saying that eating too much meat is not good for you. I eat a big breakfast. My appetite is okay. I take vitamin supplements to make sure I get what I need. How's that? I guess my diet is pretty well balanced, as well balanced as the next guy's.

How about your thoughts?

My thoughts?

Yes. Are your thoughts positive and life-affirming, or are they negative and toxic?

Toxic thoughts?

Oh, yes. Like poison. Now, about your feelings. Do you feel alive and vibrant? Do you realize how special you are? Do you look forward to each new day with hope and enthusiasm?

What does that have to do with balanced health?

Lots. I'll get into that in a minute. But first, tell me about your spiritual health. Are you glad to be alive? Are you thankful for each new day? Do you feel the healing power of the universe in every cell of your wonderful body? Do you feel whole and complete?

Well, I believe in God, if that's what you mean by spiritual. Hey, haven't you gone pretty far afield? I thought I was taking a health quiz and here you are talking about thoughts and feelings and the power of the universe!

You bet! Balanced health involves all of these areas, each developed to its optimum level and all in perfect balance. Let's take them one at a time and see how they feel. First . . .

OPTIMUM PHYSICAL HEALTH

How does optimum physical health feel? Do you recall a time in your life when you felt physically great, when you were full of energy and the day did not have enough hours in it?

Well, let's see. I guess when I was about two.

Wonderful. How did you feel then?

I can't recall exactly, but I was full of energy, that's for sure. My mother used to tell me stories about how she couldn't keep up with me — terrible twos, you know. Up early, run, run, run. Into everything. Didn't want to go to bed. The whole world seemed like a playground to me. I must have been a handful.

Yeah. You must have been in top form! You were full of energy then. Do you still feel that way?

Hardly.

Would you like to feel full of energy? How about this: pop out of bed; have a productive, energy-filled day; move your body easily; relax when you want to; manage stress well; get a good night's sleep; then get up and go again!

Of course I would.

Wonderful. You're doing great, just great! Now, let's talk about...

OPTIMUM MENTAL HEALTH

When you were a child did you have hopes and dreams?

Oh, yes. I suppose all children have them.

What were yours?

I wanted to be a famous scientist. I wanted to discover the cure for cancer. I wanted to win the Nobel Prize. I wanted to be rich. I wanted to be President of the United States. Then it was time for lunch. After lunch I wanted to sail around the world on a yacht, then fly into space, then be a veterinarian, then win the Kentucky Derby and the Indianapolis 500 in the same year. That's because the Olympics weren't 'till the next year!

Is that all?

No. I kept coming up with new goals, new things I wanted to do. You should have seen my room. Full of toys. My parents were always telling me to clean it up.

I bet! Boy what an interesting life!

It was.

Was? Isn't your life as interesting and adventurous as it was then?

No. Not by a long shot. Those were just childhood dreams. Life isn't like that. There comes a time when...

Hold it! Before you go on, let me ask you some questions. Would you like your life to be a series of exciting adventures again? Would you like to expect the best that life has to offer and to achieve what you really want? Would you like to set your goals high and to reach them? Would you like to find the best solutions to any problems you might encounter!

Yes. Who wouldn't?

Great! Now on to...

OPTIMUM EMOTIONAL HEALTH

When was the last time somebody told you how wonderful you are?

Oh, come on.

When was the last time someone told you you're great?

Stop it.

You're fantastic! You're terrrrrrrific!

No, no, stop. Please stop.

You're talented! You're really something!

Enough, enough.

Are these the kinds of things you grew up hearing? Really supportive things, lots of acceptance?

Sometimes. But I always figured that if the person really knew what I was like, they wouldn't say them.

Oh? Don't you believe those things about yourself? Aren't you great? You started off perfect, unique, one of a kind. You still are, aren't you?

I wish I were. But I have lots of faults. Face it. I'm just not that great. I'm...

Hold it! How would you like to feel great about yourself, without feeling conceited? How would you like to tell yourself how terrific you are, and believe it? How would you like to be able to take an honest compliment without feeling embarrassed? How would you like to feel like a million? How about looking in a mirror and smiling at that fine person looking back at you?

Sounds good to me. Boy, I can't remember when I last did that.

Okay, fine. You will; believe me. Now, let's discuss the fourth aspect of balanced health, the part that rounds things out...

OPTIMUM SPIRITUAL HEALTH

Recall a time in your life when you felt exactly right with the universe, a time when you were thankful to be alive and an active part of humanity.

That hasn't happened very often, but I do recall one time in particular. It was when I was around twenty. Everything just seemed to fall into place for me. I was doing well in my job. I had lots of friends. I had just started dating a special person. All areas of my life were filled with excitement. I had the world by the tail. The future seemed bright!

Fine. Stay with that for a moment. Was that a time when you felt complete, whole?

Yes, indeed!

Did you feel loving, accepting, and supportive toward others?

Yeah. I wanted to share that feeling with everyone.

Were you a good friend, a loyal partner, an honest person?

Yes!

And the more you gave, the better you felt and the better you felt the more you gave. And weren't you always in the right place at the right time?

That's right!

And as you gave more and more love, didn't more and more love come back to you?

Yes, indeed!

You must have really been in touch with the universe. Every cell in your body must have tingled.

You bet!

Fantastic! Let's get that feeling back. How about let's put it all together — the physical, the mental, the emotional, and the spiritual. Let's put them in balance and optimize each aspect of your health. Let's give you the vitality and the positive mental, emotional and spiritual life that you deserve.

Yes, yes, yes! What's the secret?

Well, if there is one secret that applies to all areas of your health, it is...

TOXINS OUT, NOURISHMENT IN

Toxins are poisons;
 they tear down.

Nourishment is fuel;
 it builds up.

Toxic buildup leads to dis-ease;
 proper nourishment leads to health.

Toxic foods tear down the body;
　　proper foods build up the cells.

Toxic thoughts block goals;
　　positive thoughts bring results.

Toxic emotions bring self hatred;
　　positive feelings bring self-esteem.

Ill-will brings ill-will, multiplied;
　　love brings love, multiplied.

That all sounds so simple. If it's so easy, why doesn't everyone do it?

Beats me.

You mean to tell me that all I have to do is get toxins out and put nourishment in and I will look and feel wonderful!

Yes.

Then how do I go about doing this?

Let's go step by step, starting with the physical...

CHAPTER TWO

Achieving Optimum Physical Health

Your body is remarkable! Given the proper nourishment, it just hums along, serving you like a finely tuned sports car, taking you where you want to go in style!

I seem to have a clunker.

Oh, no you don't. See your body the way you want it to be, the way it can be, the way it will be. Don't get stuck on your body's present condition. Always see the wonderful possibilities. Turn your so-called clunker into a marvelous showpiece!

How?

First, by realizing that...

THE BODY HEALS ITSELF

You know, I was comparing the body to an automobile. But the body is better than that, more intricate, more mobile, able to do so much more for you. And on top of that, it heals itself.

It is wonderful what the body does if you give it the right tools and if you take it out for a spin regularly. Your body, if you do not abuse it, will keep itself at peak efficiency, running like a top.

If you do not mistreat it, it will not break down on you, causing those expensive repair bills. It could last for decades, even more than a century.

I am continually amazed at how wonderful the body is and how, with special care, even bodies that have been neglected and mistreated for many years have responded to loving care. I have personally witnessed thousands of people literally turn their physical health around from a state of toxicity and ill-health to a state of optimum health and vibrancy. And so can you.

If your body is out of sorts in one or more of many ways, it is due to. . .

TRAPPED TOXINS

If you neglect your car, what happens? The oil gets gritty, sludge builds up, the engine doesn't run properly, or gives out altogether. You know, it turns into a junk heap.

Same with your body. If you treat your body like a junk heap, and if you do not clean it out regularly, you get toxic build-up.

What are toxins?

Toxins are poisons. They tear down. They weaken the body.

Where do they come from?

There are toxins that you take into your body directly, such things as food additives, smoke, alcohol. The body will work very hard to rid itself of these toxins. Very hard. As anyone who has ever gotten really drunk can tell you, the body will go to great lengths to get rid of toxins. It will literally throw them up and out.

I think I know what you mean.

Besides toxins taken in from the outside, toxins are created inside the body, if it is mistreated over time. Here's how this occurs:

Your body needs fuel. You feed it. It absorbs nutrients (vitamins, minerals, trace elements, amino acids, enzymes), and gets rid of the rest (through perspiration, respiration and elimination). What happens when you take in more than the body can either use or eliminate?

You get fat.

Worse. You get fat and the excess food rots inside your body creating sludge. This sludge is sent through your blood stream to all your cells. Instead of being vibrant and alive, you become literally sluggish. And what doesn't get sent out into your blood stream gets trapped.

How do toxins get trapped?

Toxins get trapped this way: in a healthy body, needed nutrients are absorbed into the blood stream. They are pumped around the body and distributed where they are needed or are stored for later use. What happens when there is toxic build-up? The large intestine, also known as the colon, gets coated with sludge. Layer upon layer of it. The large intestine becomes impacted with this material. Some foods are really bad for this. These are the mucus foods. I will talk about them soon.

When there are several layers of impacted matter coating the large intestine, and excessive mucus coating the small intestine, it becomes harder and harder for the nutrients to pass through into the blood stream. That is why a person can eat and eat and eat and literally be starving to death. The nutrients are not getting to the cells. The body is not being nourished.

And remember, that stuff that is sitting around in there is turning into more toxins. And those toxins are just another word for poisons. Some of those poisons are being sent out into the blood stream and deposited in various parts of the body. When they build up, they weaken the cells. The body is then a breeding ground for. . .

DIS-EASE

By dis-ease you mean indigestion, heart-burn, discomfort, don't you?

By dis-ease I mean any condition of ill-health. It can be anything from the flu to cancer, from hypoglycemia to arthritis, from heart problems to depression to allergies.

You mean to say that all of these things have the same basic cause?

I am not talking about cause. What I am saying is that dis-eases do not tend to get a foothold in a healthy body, anymore than your car engine will break down if you keep it properly tuned and if you change the oil regularly.

A healthy body is a dis-ease free body. A person with optimum physical health is not a sick person.

Here's an example. When the flu is going around, some people get it and others don't. Some get it worse than others. Everyone is exposed to the flu virus, but the virus doesn't get a foothold in a healthy body. Whether or not a person is likely to get the flu has to do with the condition of the body. An optimally healthy body will not get it, that's if one's thoughts are also in optimum shape, but that's a subject we will be discussing later.

Dis-ease attacks at the weakest point. It will attack an unhealthy body, but it will tend to by-pass a healthy body.

You mean to say that if I have optimum health, I will be dis-ease free?

Yes, unless you were born with a certain predisposition to a particular dis-ease. And even then, a healthy body will minimize your chances of getting the dis-ease. And if you do get it, the symptoms will not be as severe.

But what about dis-eases that are already there?

Remember: the body heals itself.

Proper nourishment supports the body's self-healing process. I have seen it thousands of times. People with arthritis, right along with people with cancer, right next to people with allergies, sitting across from people with diabetes. I have seen people with these and many other conditions attain optimum health.

I didn't do it for them. When these people took responsibility for their own health, their own bodies did it. That's because the body is self-righting.

If toxins are trapped in the body, aren't they going to keep the body unhealthy, even with proper nutrition?

That would be true if the toxins remained in the body forever. That's why it is important to...

DETOXIFY YOUR BODY

Up to a point your body will detoxify itself. In fact, it is always in the process of getting rid of toxins. Every time you breathe out, you are getting rid of toxic gases. Every time you perspire, toxins are being released through your pores. Did you know that your skin is an organ? Yes. It is your body's largest organ and is an important organ for releasing toxins. And, of course, if you have normal elimination, your body is releasing toxins with the normal waste material.

But without your help, your body will fall behind. If you do not breathe deeply, if you do not work up a sweat, or if you are constipated, you can be certain that you are adding to the build-up of toxins in your body.

There are enough toxins taken in from the outside — car exhaust, pollution, and so forth. The body works hard enough getting rid of them. But when you add toxins to that load, watch out! For crying out loud, your body can do only so much!

I thought the body could do anything.

Not if you continue to contribute to toxic build-up. You can be your body's best friend or its worst enemy. Your body is naturally wonderful, but to achieve optimum physical health it will need your help.

My help? What can I do?

First, you can stop stuffing more into your body than

it can use or eliminate. Stop adding to the toxic build-up. Your body will love you for it.

Is that the secret to optimum physical health?

That's part of it. But remember, over the years your intestines and cells have accumulated toxins. If the diet that you told me about in the health quiz is typical of your eating habits, you have years of sludge in there — coffee, sugar, meat, milk, and probably cereals, eggs, cheese, potato chips, soft drinks, fast foods, and on and on.

If you stop adding to the sludge, your body will start to get rid of it. Your body will begin to detoxify. If you are in no great hurry and if you are fairly healthy physically, your body will do the job. And you will be rewarded with renewed energy and vigor. And, as a bonus, you will achieve your ideal weight! If you are overweight, you will get rid of weight. If you are underweight, you will gain.

Sounds good to me.

Yes. But getting rid of toxins is only part of the process. You also have to be aware of...

PHYSICAL NOURISHMENT

Well, you have decided to get the toxins out of your body and not to add more. That's great. Congratulations!

Now, what are you going to put in there? How are you going to nourish that wonderful showpiece of yours?

It's not a showpiece yet.

Remember: see the possibilities! You really are something! You are beautiful, you sly devil. You've gotta love that body, just love it!! How are you going to treat your new friend? How are you going to nourish your body?

Well, I guess I will have to starve myself until the toxic build-up gets eliminated.

Oh, no you won't. In fact, your body will get more nourishment than it has had in years! Real live nourishment. You will literally be feeding your body raw power. Your body will get all of the nourishment it needs to achieve optimum physical health. You will become a lean machine, just as you have always wanted to be!

Sounds great. Where do I start?

I'll tell you where I started. I started with two basic principles and built on them. The first principle was. . .

EAT LIVE FOR LIFE

Live foods provide nourishment to your body. All of the vitamins, minerals, trace elements, enzymes, and amino acids that live foods contain are available to your body. Your optimally healthy body will convert them to pure energy. By eating live foods, you are working with your body, not against it. For optimum physical health, I began by eating live foods, optimal foods.

Optimal foods?

Yes. Optimal foods are...

...ORGANICALLY GROWN. If at all possible, eat organically grown foods. They have more nutrients than do chemicalized foods and they do not have those toxins that you have decided not to put into your body.

...FRESH. Fruit, vegetables, sprouts and seeds should be eaten as fresh as possible. Precious nutrients are lost with the passage of time.

...MINIMALLY PROCESSED. Processing foods destroys their energy value. Heat is the worst culprit. Heat destroys enzymes, vitamins, minerals, and amino acids. Freezing is not as damaging because the enzymes survive. Dehydration at low temperature keeps most of the nutrients intact, except water soluble ones. The least damaging form of processing is mechanical (chopping, shredding, etc.) Juicing is a good process because your body can absorb juices more easily than it can whole foods.

Remember: the more that food is processed, the less it has to offer your body. Eat your foods live for life. That's the first principle. The second is the principle of . . .

PROPER FOOD COMBINING

In order for your body to get the nutrients that live foods offer, the foods must be broken down and liquified. Most of this is done in your stomach, the mixing-bowl of your body. As you know, the stomach churns the food, mixes it with enzymes, and breaks it down into a liquid. Then sends this liquid on to the small intestine.

Well, that's pretty basic. But what does that have to do with food combining?

Different foods spend different amounts of time in the stomach and require different digestive juices. Some require an acid digestion; others require an alkaline digestion. You do not want to mix those foods. If the stomach is to do its job quickly and efficiently, you should eat foods that are compatible with each other, foods that require the same type of digestion. The point is to get the food into and out of your stomach quickly and efficiently.

What's the rush?

Let's take a break. There's something outside that I want to show you...

...Boy, is it hot out here! It must be almost 100°.

Yes. In fact, it's 98.6° out here. Now, see that plate over there, the one with the fruit and the ground meat on it?

I don't have to look. I can smell them, especially that meat. Whew!!

I placed that plate out here a few hours ago, to demonstrate to you what happens when food sits around at 98.6°, your body temperature.

Okay, okay. Let's go in now. You've made your point...

...Now, why don't you want food to rot inside your body?

Because if it rots, it turns into toxic material, which leads to toxic build-up.

You've got it. You are learning fast. Good for you!

So it pays to use your stomach efficiently, and to do that, you should follow the principle of proper food combining. Your bod will love you for it! Your stomach will be grateful!

That sounds good in theory. But what goes with what?

Okay. Let me tell you...

HOW TO COMBINE YOUR FOODS PROPERLY

There are five rules to follow in proper food combining. Following these rules will allow your stomach to do its job efficiently.

Rule 1: Liquids alone. Do not drink liquids with your meals unless that is all you are having at that meal, and that includes water. Water dilutes the digestive juices in your stomach, making digestion less efficient.

How am I going to wash my food down, then?

By chewing it thoroughly. You will secrete saliva which will aid digestion as well as help the food get down your esophagus. Do not gulp your food.

Rule 2: Do not mix protein foods (nuts, seeds, olives, avocado, coconuts, etc.) with starchy foods (grains, beans, squash, potatoes, etc.) in the same meal. You may, however, mix either of them with vegetables and sprouts.

Rule 3: Fruits alone. Do not use fruit as an appetizer or a dessert. Fruit stays in your stomach for 30 to 60 minutes. When you eat fruit, do so about an hour before eating other foods.

You mean that fruits are not compatible with other foods?

Not as far as your stomach is concerned. When you consider the time that fruit stays in the stomach and the types of enzymes needed to break fruits down, they should be eaten by themselves. Not only that, some fruits are not compatible with others. That brings us to:

Rule 4: Acid fruit or sweet fruit plus sub-acid fruit.

In other words, do not mix acid fruit and sweet fruit in the same meal.

Which fruits are which?

The acid fruits are on the sour side — oranges, lemons, limes, grapefruit, cranberries, strawberries, pineapple, pomegranates.

The sweet fruits are such things as bananas, dates, figs, prunes, raisins, persimmons, and so forth.

The sub-acid fruits are in between — apples, apricots, cherries, grapes, peaches, pears, payaya, mangoes, etc.

Optimally, one should go easy on the sweet fruits; they contain too much sugar. But in no case is it wise to mix acid fruits with sweet fruits or fruits of any kind with anything else.

Rule 5: Melons alone. Melons, like fruit, should not be eaten as a dessert. You might want to eat melons for breakfast, but do not eat watermelon with other melons.

Why eat melons alone? And why not mix watermelon with other melons?

That brings us back to the theory of food combining. Recall that different foods spend different amounts of time in the stomach and require different enzymes. For the greatest efficiency you do not want more than one type of food in your stomach at the same time. Watermelon needs very little digestion. It is mostly water and passes through the stomach quickly. Other melons take slightly longer to digest, while other foods take longer still. Your stomach will do its best for you if it works on one type of food at a time.

Okay. Let's see if I've got it.

Rule 1: Liquids alone.

Right.

Rule 2: Proteins or starches, not both, with vegetables.

Great.

Rule 3: Fruit alone.

Correct.

Rule 4: Do not mix acid fruits with sweet fruits.

Excellent!

Rule 5: Melons alone and do not mix watermelon with other melons.

A+, you've got it!

*Great! You know, you are talking about optimum this
and optimum that. Is there an optimum optimum food?*

I was waiting for you to ask that. Now you are talking
my language. The best, the optimum food of the optimum
foods is...

WHEATGRASS

Wheatgrass? You mean grass as in lawn?

I mean grass as in trays. I mean grass grown from
wheat, the hard, winter wheat berries, then juiced and
taken fresh. Great stuff, that wheatgrass juice. It is the
optimum optimum. It is the cat's meow. It's incredible!

What's so good about it?

Now you've got me started. Watch out!

Wheatgrass juice:
  ...Is a fine natural source of chlorophyll.
  Chlorophyll provides energy for your cells. The

molecular structure of chlorophyll is similar to that of hemoglobin.

...Contains hundreds of enzymes, essential for digestion.

...Contains all eight essential amino acids plus many other amino acids that the body itself manufactures.

...Is high in vitamins C, the B vitamins, vitamin E and carotene.

...Is a good source of minerals and trace elements needed by the body.

...Is a complete food.

...Is cleansing.

...Encourages the growth of intestinal flora, those friendly bacteria that fight dis-ease.

...Provides instant energy.

...Is the best single food anywhere!

Wheatgrass juice helps your body's self-healing process.

That's quite a claim.

I've seen the results. I use it myself and I've personally seen thousands of people benefit from it. Ever since I learned about it from Ann Wigmore, who really popularized it, I have been sold on it. It is a key part of optimum physical health. Try it; you'll love it! Try it for one month, and if you are not completely satisfied...

What is this? A sales pitch?

Yes.

Okay. I'll try it. How do I get some?

You can grow it yourself in trays or in a hydroponic unit. There are books to show you how. Here are two: THE WHEATGRASS BOOK by Ann Wigmore and SURVIVAL INTO THE 21ST CENTURY by Viktoras Kulvinskas.

Some health food stores are beginning to provide fresh wheatgrass juice. If your favorite store doesn't have it freshly juiced, ask them to look into it. There really is a growing interest in wheatgrass, as well there should be!

How much of it do you drink?

At first I drank 6 ounces a day, 3 ounces in the morning and 3 ounces in the afternoon. Now I drink 3 ounces a day, in the morning.

Besides wheatgrass juice, are there any other foods that are really good for you?

Yes...

FERMENTED FOODS

Fermented foods aid digestion. They are considered pre-digested foods, so they are easily assimilated into the intestines. Fermented foods are also rich in B vitamins and are full of enzymes. As a bonus, natural lactic acid is produced during the fermentation process.

Fermented foods encourage the growth of intestinal flora, those friendly bacteria that fight the bad guys, the harmful bacteria. The gunfight at the O.K. Corral is fought each day in your intestinal tract. You want the good guys to win. Fermented foods build up their strength so that they will have a quick draw.

By fermented foods do you mean stuff like beer? I wouldn't think that you would encourage the use of alcohol.

I don't. I am talking about fermented foods without alcohol. You are familiar with sauerkraut. Made without salt it is excellent for you. But have you heard of rejuvelac?

Rejuvelac?

Yes. It also aids digestion and it is a fine source of B vitamins. To make it, soak one part soft spring wheat berries in 3 parts purified water for 24 hours. Then pour off the water into a jar. That soak water is rejuvelac. Drinking a quart of it a day helps keep digestive problems away!

Fermented foods are excellent and versatile. And so are. . .

SPROUTS

Sprouts are coming into their own. That is wonderful. They are convenient, nutritious and an aid to detoxification.

I know they are convenient. Most salad bars have

them. Many grocery stores stock them. They are easy to grow at home. Almost everyone has eaten them. I know they are good for you, but I don't exactly know why.

Eating sprouts is like eating a bite of life itself! All of the wonderful vitamins, especially the B vitamins, and the amino acids, minerals, enzymes and chlorophyll just pop out of the sprout and into your mouth ready to go.

Why not just eat the seeds?

That's fine, too. But sprouted seeds and legumes are a pre-digested food. That means that they are easy for your body to assimilate. The starches have been broken down into simple sugars, ready to provide your body with energy. Alfalfa, sunflower and buckwheat sprouts are great for nutrition, but the others are valuable, too.

You say that sprouts aid detoxification. Which sprouts have you found to be best for that?

Alfalfa, mung beans, lentils and fenugreek.

Fenugreek?

Fenugreek is a legume. The sprouts help cleanse the kidneys, pancreas and liver. And they also assist in eliminating toxins through the skin, that big, wrap-around organ.

A combination of these sprouts will supply your body with much of the raw energy that it needs, while helping it get rid of those unwanted toxins.

Remember: Wheatgrass, fermented foods, sprouts — the optimum of the optimum foods.

What about bad, bad foods. What foods do you love to hate?

I don't love to hate anything. That's something we will be taking up later. But I do not eat...

MEAT AND DAIRY PRODUCTS

I've cut down on my meat consumption, but what do I tell my friends when they tell me that I am not getting my protein?

You are getting plenty of protein. When you are talking about protein, you are talking about amino acids, usable protein. There are eight amino acids that are considered the most essential. These eight and many more, are provided in your raw foods, especially wheatgrass juice and alfalfa sprouts. There is no need to worry about not getting your protein.

Now let's look at what your friends are getting in their meat. They are getting uric acid, which is hard on the kidneys. They are getting lots of hormones, which are used to speed up the growth of beef, pork, chicken and other flesh foods, harmful hormones. They are getting the chemicals used to preserve the meat. These are toxins.

In addition, meat is served cooked. That destroys the enzymes and most of the nutrients.

Not only that, meat stays in the stomach for a long time, up to four or five times as long as fruits and vegetables. And that's if it is eaten alone. If it is combined with other foods, it is there longer and you already know what that means.

Toxins.

Right! I do not need the toxic side effects of meat. I do not eat it. Nor do I consume dairy products.

Why not? I always thought that milk was necessary for strong bones and teeth. You know, the calcium.

Calcium. You want calcium, so eat sesame seeds. They are loaded with calcium. Your fruits and vegetables, especially green vegetables and members of the cabbage family also contain calcium. No need to worry about that.

Now, let's look at the other side of dairy products, what they do **to** you, not **for** you. Dairy products are mucus forming. Mucus as in stopped-up nose. Mucus as in glued-up intestines. Normally, mucus coats the intestines to protect them. When your intestines are coated with excessive mucus, though, it is harder for the nutrients to enter your blood stream. Excessive mucus is like glue. It plugs. It adds to toxic build-up. It traps sludge inside your body.

I avoid meat and dairy products. But I certainly do not avoid what many people love to avoid, and that is . . .

EXERCISE

Getting back to that sports car. You can tune it up, change the oil, give it a major overhaul, but if it sits around doing nothing, it will be sluggish. If you have ever driven a car that has been sitting around for a few months, you know what I mean — sputter, cough. You have to take it out for a spin regularly, and not just around town. If you do not want carbon build-up, you have to take it out on the freeway.

Same with your body. You have to give it exercise. In order for your body to get all of those nutrients that you are starting to give it, they have to be distributed. That means that your blood has to circulate. Your heart has to pump it around. The best way to get your heart pumping is through exercise, aerobic exercise. It doesn't take long. A little each day. Work up a sweat. Get that heart pumping.

Exercise is also great for detoxification. Recall that your body gets rid of toxins through the skin. How do you work up a sweat? Exercise.

Your lungs get rid of toxic gases when you breathe out. The deeper you breathe, the more toxins are released when you exhale. Breathe deeply when you exercise.

And here is one that most people have not heard about, but it is really important: lymph. Toxins in your cells, when released, are washed away by your lymphatic system. Lymph fluid circulates throughout your body carrying these toxins away. But unlike your circulatory system, your lymphatic system has no pump. You have to move that lymph fluid around your body. How do you do that?

Exercise. Aerobic exercise.

Is there a particular type of aerobic exercise that is best?

Rebounding. It is not necessarily the best aerobic exercise, but it is easy, concentrated and fun!

Do you remember when you were a child and you bounced on the bed or on the couch?

Sure I do. That was fun. But when I got caught I was usually punished.

Well, rebounding is like that, except that instead of getting punished, you are rewarded! As your physical health is on the rebound, you will benefit from being on the rebounder.

What is a rebounder?

It is a mini-trampoline. It is small, lightweight, and easy to use. A few minutes on one of those and your body will be humming. It is like a fifty mile drive on the freeway is to your newly restored automobile! Here, would you like to try my rebounder?

Sure!

Okay. Take off your shoes and bounce. When you're

finished, I want to start talking about the other aspects of optimum health. I have a wonderful technique to share with you.

Okay. One...two...three...bounce!!

CHAPTER THREE

Alpha

Hey, kiddo! What are you doing up there on that cloud?

I don't know, Raychel. I was bouncing on the rebounder and I guess I got carried away. That was great fun!

You don't have to bounce so high. Repetitions are the key. But since you are up there, I'll come up and join you...

..How did you get up here?

I sort of beamed myself up. I used the fantastic powers of my mind.

Boy, you must have some brain!

Yes. And so do you. While we are up here where it's soft and comfortable, let me tell you about...

THE POWER OF THE MIND

Grab a wisp of pillowy cloud and relax. There, that's good. Ready?

Go ahead.

Do you know how wonderful your mind is, how powerful? Do you know that you have the power to create health, happiness, abundance in your life?

I do?

Oh, yes. You have a terrific mind. Billions and billions of brain cells, each working with the others to create your wonderful intelligence. And that intelligence is electromagnetic energy which is sent out and connected to other people's intelligence. And all of that intelligence is mighty powerful!

Sounds kind of weird to me, sort of like telepathy or something.

Have you ever thought about someone you hadn't seen for a long time, then the phone rang and it was that person?

Yes. But that was just a coincidence.

No it wasn't. You see, so little is actually known about

the power of the mind. It is considered the last frontier. But there is so much power there, it's incredible!

How do you know?

I've seen it. Over and over. I've seen the results of tapping the power of the mind. I have tapped that power myself. I do it every day. And I get results.

What results?

Results like instant relaxation, pain control, restful sleep, and much more.

I wish I could relax more. I'm under a lot of pressure.

You will be able to relax. Instantly! Boy, are you in for a treat! You will be amazed at the results when you learn how to reach your subconscious mind. Not just relaxation, but physical, mental, emotional, spiritual well-being, balanced health.

Subconscious mind?

I will explain it this way: There is the conscious mind and the subconscious mind. You've heard that, haven't you?

Yes. But I am not sure what the different between them is.

The conscious mind is that part of your mind that

tosses ideas, plans, alternatives around. Your subconscious mind is creative. It comes up with solutions, has flashes of insight, carries out orders sent to it by the conscious mind. It attracts things to you like a magnet. Whatever we focus on, we attract to ourselves through an electromagnetic force. It is like this:

CONSCIOUS MIND: Well, I don't know. Maybe this. No, perhaps that. But if that, then what will happen? I'll have to figure that out. Get more information. No, I can't do that...

SUBCONSCIOUS MIND: Look! Decide already! I don't want to argue with you. Make up your part of the mind and let me get to work on it. Whatever you want, I'll attract to you, but stop trying to argue with me!

Your subconscious mind will not argue with you. What you tell it will be accepted uncritically and carried out. If you want to get the job done, talk to your subconscious mind.

How?

The technique I use is called Alpha.

So tell me...

WHAT IS ALPHA?

You've heard of brain waves, haven't you?

Yes.

Well, brainwaves are measured in cycles per second. From 14 to 28 cycles per second, and even up to 50 or 60 cycles per second, we call Beta. That's when your mind is really active. Your conscious mind is at work, thinking thousands of thoughts, tossing things around, gathering information, trying to force thoughts into place.

But if you slow your brain activity down to 7 to 14 cycles per second, you are in Alpha. When you are at the Alpha level you are more relaxed and receptive. And you are also more aware and in-tune with your subconscious mind.

If you slow your brain waves down to $3\frac{1}{2}$ to 7 cycles per second, you enter Theta, a state of deep meditation. The Theta level is the inspirational level of mind. It is at that level where you are at your most creative.

The deepest level of mind, with brain waves of $\frac{1}{2}$ to $3\frac{1}{2}$ cycles per second, is the Delta level, the unconscious level.

We are mainly concerned with getting to the Alpha level, where we have direct access to the subconscious mind. And while there, we also have access to the Theta level, where flashes of insight become available to us.

Sounds to me like bio-feedback.

Yes. Bio-feedback is a method of monitoring the Alpha level. If it is helpful for you, use it. But did you know that you enter Alpha, Theta, and Delta every day?

I do?

Oh, yes. When you sleep, your mind is moving from level to level. The brain waves are slowing down and speeding up throughout the night. Your mind is very busy, especially your subconscious mind. Have you ever gone to bed with a problem and awakened with the solution, "presto!"?

Sure. In fact, if I have a big decision to make, I usually sleep on it. The answer often comes to me by the time I wake up, or sometimes in the middle of the night.

That's quite common. Your conscious mind is not arguing with you, so your subconscious mind can do its thing. It pays to get in touch with your subconscious mind.

I wish I could do that when I am awake.

You can. Anytime. It's easy, relaxing and fun. You can access your subconscious mind and you can actually program yourself for health, success, happiness, whatever your conscious mind chooses.

Program?! Hold it right there. What is this, 1984?

No. 1984 has passed. You are still here, aren't you? You are alive. You have feelings. You can think all kinds of thoughts. You don't need big brother to tell you how or what to think. Always remember. . .

YOU ARE IN CONTROL

And you do not need me to tell you what to think. What you think is up to you and you alone. You can accept or reject anything I say at any time at any level of mind.

You are in control of your own mind. I am in control of my mind. Let's get that straight right now. Okay? I don't want power over you. I only encourage you to tap the wonderful power of your own mind. Take it or leave it. It is entirely up to you.

Well, okay. I'll give it a try. I guess I will have to trust you. But don't try any funny stuff.

You don't have to trust me. Remember: you can

accept or reject anything I say at any level of mind. I have absolutely no power over you whatsoever.

Okay. . .

HOW DO I GET INTO ALPHA?

First, let's get comfortable. I usually sit in a comfortable chair, my legs uncrossed, my hands on my lap. But since we are up here, let's just lean back. Could you hand me that cloud over there, that puffy one? Yes, that one. Thanks. Ah, that's good. Shall we get started?

Ready.

Take a deep breath and imagine the color red. This will alert you to relax. As you breathe out, mentally repeat the word "relax" several times.

Relax
  Relax
    Relax

Good. You are doing fine.

Now, to enter a deeper, healthier level of mind, take another deep breath and imagine the color purple. As you breathe out, mentally repeat the word "healthier" several times.

> Healthier
> > Healthier
> > > Healthier

Wonderful. You are entering a deeper, healthier level of mind.

To enter an even deeper, healthier level of mind, take another deep breath and imagine the color blue. As you breathe out, mentally repeat the word "deeper" several times.

> Deeper
> > Deeper
> > > Deeper

Fine. You're doing fine.

Now, let's go into a deeper, even healthier level of mind. I will count from 20 down to 10. With every descending number you will **feel** yourself entering a deeper, healthier level of mind and you **will** enter a deeper, healthier level of mind.

20...
  19...
    18...

Feel yourself going deeper and deeper with each breath you take.

17...
  16...
    15...

Deeper and deeper, healthier and healthier.

14...
  13...
    12...

More and more relaxed.

11...
  10...

You are now at a deeper, healthier level than before.

Now, let's go to an even deeper, healthier level of mind.

Focus on your hands and arms. Imagine your hands and arms completely relaxed. Place this area of your body into a deep state of relaxation.

Imagine your forehead and eyelids completely relaxed. Good. Good.

Imagine your mouth and jaw completely relaxed. Fine.

Now your neck and shoulders. Excellent!

Take a deep breath and relax your chest. Super!

Relax your stomach. Release all tension and pressures in this area. Now relax your chest and stomach internally. Relax all organs,
    all glands,
        all cells.

Allow them to function in a normal, rhythmic, healthy manner.

Marvelous!

Relax your hips. . .
    legs. . .
        calves. . .
            ankles
                fine.

Relax your feet and toes. . .

Great! Great! You're doing great!

Now relax your body completely, from the top of your head all the way down to your toes.

Feel a deep sense of relaxation spread
    slowly...
        downward...
            throughout...
                your...
                    body...
                        nice!

Now even deeper and healthier.

Count from 3 down to 1. Feel how nice it is to be here on this cloud.

Relax.

    Three...
        nice...
            soft...
                comfortable...

    Two...
        peaceful...
            serene...

    One.

Now you are at the Alpha level. It is a very pleasant feeling to be deeply relaxed. Feel the peacefulness. Good. Feel the serenity...fine.

Feel yourself getting. . .
better and better. . .
healthier and healthier!

Every time you enter the Alpha level of mind, you will enter a deeper, healthier level of mind faster and easier than ever before.

Now, let's stay at this level for awhile. It feels good. It feels. . .
. . . peaceful
. . . serene,
. . . healthy,
. . . relaxed.

While at the Alpha level of mind, program your subconscious mind for. . .
. . . optimum health.
. . . success.
. . . better relationships.
. . . joy.
. . . inner peace.
. . . the best of everything for everybody.

Now I will stop talking for a few minutes. You are alone with your thoughts. . .

Alone with your thoughts. . .

Okay. when you are ready, come back up to the conscious level. When you do, you will be wide awake, feeling healthier and better than before. And you will hand me the keys to your car...

How do you feel?

Wonderful! But no way am I going to give you my car keys. I knew you'd try to pull something!

You see! You are in control. You can accept or reject anything I say at any level of mind.

Tricky! Listen. Isn't this like hypnosis?

No. Alpha is autogenics, self-programming. You are always, at every moment, in control. You can use it whenever you want to access your subconscious mind.

Does it always take this long? I am a busy person.

Oh, no. Every time you do it, it gets faster and easier. In fact, after a few times, you can achieve...

INSTANT RELAXATION

Sometimes one needs to get to the Alpha level in a hurry, especially in a stressful situation when a person needs to be calm.

An example that comes to my mind is when one of my former students was taking his final exams in graduate school. When he sat down to take the exam, his mind went blank. He looked at the questions and froze. He was just about to walk out of the exam and give up, when he remembered the technique that I am going to share with you now. It's called the three-finger technique.

He immediately went to the Alpha level, took a deep breath, got in touch with his subconscious mind, and took the exam. Not only did he pass the examination, but he scored in the top 10% of the class!

That's great! I find myself in stressful situations fairly often. How do I use the three-finger technique?

Start by going into Alpha the regular way.
  Red. . .relax
    Purple. . .healthier
      Blue. . .deeper
        20 down to 10
          Hands and arms. . .forehead. . .mouth
            and jaw. . .neck and shoulders. . .

chest...stomach...glands..
cells...hips...legs...calves...
ankles...feet...toes...
whole body.
Three...two...one...
Alpha!

Now, form a circle with your right thumb and the first two fingers of your right hand. That's right. Touch the tips of your index and middle fingers with the tip of your thumb. You've got it. Now the same with your left hand.

You have made a conscious-unconscious connection. You have completed a circuit. You will use this three-finger technique to achieve instant relaxation.

While you are here at the Alpha level, program your subconscious mind to achieve instant relaxation. Whenever you complete the circuit using the three-finger technique, you will enter the Alpha level, feeling relaxed, peaceful and serene. You will be at your ideal place of relaxation. There will no longer be a need to go through the regular procedure to get to the Alpha level. You will be able to do it simply by using the three-finger connection.

Now, I will meet you back at the conscious level...

...Hi. How do you feel now?

I feel really good. But to be honest with you, I don't think I've quite got it yet. I put my fingers together and I do not go as deep as I do the regular, slower way.

That's fine. Keep practicing. You will get it. Don't be concerned. Go into Alpha the regular way a few more times while practicing the three-finger technique. And since you have programmed both hands, you will be able to use either the right or the left. You will do it. I know you will.

While we are at it, how can I use Alpha, besides just to relax?

How about...

PAIN CONTROL

To program yourself for pain control, go to the Alpha level, either through the standard method or by using the three-finger technique.

Now imagine your right hand being very cold. Very,

very cold. Next time you have a pain, place that hand over the part of the body that hurts and repeat the word "gone" several times.

> Gone...
>   Gone...
>   Gone...

You will be practicing mental anesthesia. The discomfort will subside very quickly!

To remove the coldness from your hand. Simply take your left hand and draw the cold from the back of your right hand toward the fingers a couple of times...until it feels normal again.

Wait a minute! Come on! When I have a pain I don't have time to go into Alpha. How do you expect me to relax when I have a sharp pain?

I don't. Once you have programmed your mind for pain control, it is programmed. Give your subconscious mind the "gone" instruction and it will respond immediately when the need arises.

The first few times you might have to use the cold hand technique. After that, all you will have to do is say "gone" and your subconscious mind will do the work.

You mean to say it's that easy?

Yes. remember, you are tapping the power of the mind, and that power is awesome. Your mind is so powerful that you can actually use this technique to help others, too.

How?

Let me tell you a little story about this technique. It is hard to believe, but it is true!

I once had a 1957 T-Bird, one of those little cars with no back seat. I was going somewhere with two friends, so my friend, Esther, had to sit on the other friend's lap. When they were squeezing into the car, the person on the bottom slammed the car door, right on Esther's fingers!

Ouch!!!!!

Now, get this. I could actually see Esther's hand caught in the car door. I saw it with my own eyes.

Immediately, I said "gone!"

When the car door was opened, we looked at the hand. There was no visible damage, nor was there any pain! Don't ask me how it works. I can't tell you. I don't know. I just know it did work then and it works whenever I use it. I look at the results. I have seen it work for hundreds of people hundreds of times, though not all as dramatically as the time in the T-Bird.

And, by the way, Esther was a pianist!

Wow! That's really something. What other ways can I use Alpha?

Many ways. For example. . .

REACH!

This one is fun. It's called "reach!"

I'm certain there have been times when you have thought you lost something. Car keys are common.

Yes. Most everybody has, I'm sure.

Well, let me tell you, nothing is ever lost. You might be temporarily separated from something, but it is not lost. Now this technique is amazing. I have seen it work so many times.

You know how you feel when you think you have lost something important.

I usually go into a panic, especially if I really need it.

Right. Your conscious mind is very active. Where did I put it? Where was I? You retrace your steps; you worry; you fret. Why not let your subconscious mind find it? Here's how:

Next time you go into Alpha, program your mind for reach! That instruction will tell your subconscious to get to work on locating the object. Remember: once you have programmed your subconscious mind, it is there. You do not have to reprogram it for that task.

Now, from now on, when you want to locate something, think of the object. Say "reach!" If you choose, you can even extend your arm and literally reach out. Repeat this a couple of times, then put it out of your mind. Just forget about the object. The results will amaze you!

This I've got to see.

Don't believe me. Try it. I'm telling you, it works. It has worked for hundreds of my students. I recall one in particular. Let's call her Judy.

Judy came to me very upset. She had lost her contact lenses and she did not have a spare pair or regular eyeglasses. Without them, she was literally lost. She had enlisted several people to look for them, but with no luck.

When she came to me she was in a panic, of course.

I suggested she try the reach! technique. She did, then she went to her room to relax. As she relaxed, one of her hands sliped to the edge of the mattress. She felt something on her fingers and when she checked, not one, but both of her contacts were there!

Oh, come on!

I'm telling you. It happened. And I have seen this technique work many many times. I use it myself. And anyway, what do you have to lose that you haven't already lost, if you believe you can lose things?

I guess you're right there. I'll try it. What other goodies do you have for me?

It's been a long day. How about getting some sleep?

I could use some, but I sometimes have trouble getting to sleep. When I do, I usually take sleeping medication.

How about trying. . .

THE SLEEP TECHNIQUE

What do I do?

When you go to bed, close your eyes, go to the Alpha level, and imagine yourself in front of a chalkboard. Have an imaginary piece of chalk in one hand and an eraser in the other.

Mentally draw a large circle on the chalkboard. Inside the circle draw a large square.

Now erase the square, being careful not to touch the circle.

Beneath the circle, write the word "deeper" and take a deep breath. Then write the number "100" inside the circle.

Erase the number and write the word "deeper" below the other "deeper," a little smaller than the first one.

Take another deep breath. Don't rush it. Remember, the harder you try to fall asleep, the harder sleep becomes. Let sleep come naturally.

Now write the number "99" in the circle. Erase it and write the word "deeper" again, under the other "deepers" and smaller yet.

Repeat this process, slowly, until you have entered normal, natural, healthy sleep.

What you are doing is blocking out whatever it is that prohibits you from going to sleep. When you use this method, you will awaken at your normal time, feeling refreshed, alert, and ready to go.

Ready to try it?

Yes. I hope it works.

It will. Give it some practice. It won't take long. Meanwhile, I have a few things to do. When you wake up, let's talk about optimum mental health.

Okay. 100...deeper...99...deeeeeeper...98...

CHAPTER FOUR

Achieving Optimum Mental Health

Good morning! Did you get a good night's sleep?

Better than ever. I think I'm starting to get the hang of this Alpha. Let's get going. There are only so many minutes in a day, you know.

There are more minutes than you might have thought. Every day, you are provided with 1,440 minutes. Think about it. One thousand, four hundred and forty minutes! That's quite a few.

Now, let's say that you are awake for 16 hours today, that's nearly one thousand minutes. And let's say that during each of those minutes you consciously think ten thoughts. Almost ten thousand thoughts in one day! Wow!! And each of those thoughts is stored in your memory bank.

Memory bank?

Yes. Did you know that your brain is composed of literally billions of cells? And each of those cells is capable of storing one to two million bits of information. What a computer! Everything you have ever thought or experienced is stored there in your memory bank.

Not only that, but your subconscious mind has access to all of that information. And it uses that information to solve problems, to come up with creative solutions and to carry out instructions sent to it by your conscious mind.

But remember: the subconscious mind is uncritical. It does not argue. It believes what you tell it. It is your conscious mind that chooses.

CONSCIOUS MIND: I'll have some wheatgrass juice.

SUBCONSCIOUS MIND: Okay, I'll get your body to get you some.

CONSCIOUS MIND: No. I think I'd rather have a soft drink.

SUBCONSCIOUS MIND: Okay. I'll get your body to get you that instead.

CONSCIOUS MIND: Aren't you going to stop me?

SUBCONSCIOUS MIND: No. It's your choice.

What you put in, you get out. Sometimes immediately, sometimes not for years. That's because thoughts are like seeds.

What do you mean?

I mean...

THOUGHTS MANIFEST THEMSELVES

Let's continue the above example.

CONSCIOUS MIND: Okay. I'll have the wheatgrass juice. It's good for me.

At this point the subconscious mind sends electromagnetic energy out to the body. The body responds by getting up, juicing the wheatgrass and drinking it.

It's that simple?

Well, that was a simple example. But that's the way it works. Here's another example:

Let's say that someone has been told all of his life that he is just like his dad. He has been told this often and for a long time. He even tells himself that. He has planted the seed, "I am just like my dad."

He starts to walk like his dad, talk like his dad, pick up his dad's habits. He even starts looking and thinking more like his dad. I'm sure you have seen this in operation.

Now that I think about it, yes I have. That's where they get the expressions, "He's a chip off the old block," and "Like father, like son."

You've got it. And the more he tells himself that, the more he becomes like his dad. The more he resembles his dad, the more that people comment on the resemblance. The more the comments, the greater the resemblance, and so on.

I see. The thought really begins to manifest itself in his experience.

Yes. Now let's look at both sides of this. I've got good news and bad news. Which do you want first?

Let me have the down side first. I want to end on an up note.

Fine. The down side is that..

NEGATIVE THOUGHTS BRING
NEGATIVE RESULTS

As it turns out, this young man's father died at an early age, of a heart attack.

That's terrible!

Yes. It was hard on everyone, especially our friend. You know what he told himself?

I can imagine. "My dad died of a heart attack at a young age. I'm just like him. I am afraid that I will also die that way."

Well, he could have told himself that. I am sure that many people in similar circumstances do. And when they do, they are watering those seeds and the seeds grow and you know what happens. They continue in the same physical and mental patterns that led to the father's premature death. And as a result, what they fear comes upon them.

It's not just true of heart attacks or fathers and sons, is it?

No. Not by a long shot. Whenever we have a negative thought we send a message to our subconscious. Our subconscious mind then gets to work on it.

If you tell yourself you are fat, you will be fat. If you tell yourself you can't do something, you will not be able to do it. If you concentrate on a problem, sure enough, it will grow. You can make a really huge, menacing problem out of it if you concentrate hard enough on it.

Do you mean that you become what you think?

Yes. You are the sum total of your thoughts because your thoughts manifest themselves. Our friend could have given himself a heart attack. That would have been tragic. He had so many goals he wanted to achieve. If he had continued the pattern, he never would have achieved them.

Fortunately, when his father died, our friend took stock in himself. His father's untimely death shook him up. After some soul searching he began to realize that...

POSITIVE THOUGHTS BRING POSITIVE RESULTS

Our friend decided to change the pattern. He started to think positively. And he achieved positive results. He took charge of his own life. He became his own person.

Instead of saying, "I will probably die young," he said, "I am healthy. I will live a long, happy, successful, life." He began to develop a healthy, productive lifestyle. He turned his life around.

The power of positive thinking.

Yes, Sir. Look around you. People who are successful have a positive mental attitude. They expect the best of themselves and they get positive results. They set goals and they achieve them. Time after time. What it comes down to is this:

What you can conceive and believe, you can achieve!

Again:

What you can conceive and believe, you can achieve!

Set a goal. Believe you can attain it. Go for it. You will achieve it. No matter what the goal is. Attain your ideal weight? **Sure!** Reach a million? **Of course!** Be a best-selling author? **Yes, indeed!** Direct a health institute at the age of 74? **Why not?!!**

Conceive it!

Believe it!

Achieve it!

One super goal setter and achiever is Dr. Mark Victor Hansen, author of **Future Diary.** Dr. Hansen has more than 400 pages of goals and when he accomplishes a goal he writes the word "victory" next to it.

One of his goals was to have his own televison show. He did not have the money to finance it, nor the contacts to get it on the air. But he wrote that goal down, gave it to his subconscious mind, and believed it would become a reality.

A few years later, seemingly out of the blue, he was invited by a cable television company to do the **Mark Victor Hansen Show.** Dr. Hansen was not surprised. He conceived it; he believed it; he achieved it!

But I am surrounded by negative thoughts and statements. People often say such things as, "Don't kid yourself. Be realistic. You can't do that. You are a dreamer. Come back down to earth."

You've just got to continue to dream. Dare to dream. Dare to believe. Dare to achieve! It's your choice.

Look at it this way. Your mind is capable of holding only one conscious thought at a time. You have a choice. Do you want that thought to be positive, affirmative and productive? Or do you want it to be negative and destructive? It is up to you. Remember, negative thoughts lead to negative results. Positive thoughts lead to positive results.

Of course, I would rather hold positive thoughts than negative ones. But negative thoughts keep popping up. What do I do about that?

Take control of your own mind. Take command of your computer. When you hear something you do not want to be part of your consciousness, just...

CANCEL! CANCEL!

Just like any computer, if you do not want information to be entered, you cancel it, erase it. Remember, what you put into your computer is what you get out of it. Garbage in, garbage out. Garbage to your mind is like sludge to your body — toxic.

How do I cancel unwanted information?

Easy. When you find yourself thinking negative thoughts or having doubts and fears, simply say, "Cancel!

87

Cancel!" That will be an instruction to your subconscious mind to disregard that thought. It works.

But I can't always help it. I hear people saying negative things all the time. There are lots of negative people out there.

Don't hang around with them, then. Why waste your time? Remember, you have only 1,440 minutes in a day. Why spend them being put down or held back?

Listen, you are terrific! I suggest you do not let anyone tell you any different. And I also would encourage you not to tell yourself any different.

I'm not that great. At least not yet.

Cancel! Cancel! See the beauty in yourself. See those wonderful possibilities. See yourself as you are unfolding. If you have spent your life putting yourself down, thinking you are less than wonderful, I have a suggestion. Start detoxifying your thoughts right now.

How do I do that when the thoughts are stored in my memory bank?

Try this. . .

USE ALPHA TO DETOXIFY YOUR
NEGATIVE THOUGHTS

The next time you go to the Alpha level, wait for a thought to come to the conscious level. Don't force it. Just let it come to the surface.

If the thought is a positive one, congratulate yourself for it, then let another thought emerge. And another and another, until a negative thought comes to the surface, something like, **you are unhealthy** or, **you always seem to goof things up** or, **you can't do anything right.**

When one of these thoughts emerges, say, "Cancel! Cancel!" then immediately replace that thought with a positive one.

For example, you might have been told as a youngster or for many years, that you were selfish. If you chose to believe it, it has become part of your memory bank. When you are at the Alpha level, that thought might come to the surface. If it does, try this:

NEGATIVE THOUGHT: **I am selfish. I think only of myself.**

Cancel! Cancel!

POSITIVE THOUGHT: **I always think of what is best for everyone, including myself.**

Do this as thoughts come up. Do not try to deny them. If you do, or if you try to force them, they will just go deeper into your subconscious mind. You will need to bring them to the surface in order to erase them and replace them.

This is a very powerful technique. It is like spring cleaning, deep cleaning. You are getting your mind cleared of negative thoughts that might have been there for years. You are setting the stage for positive, productive thinking.

But since some of those negative thoughts have been there for so long, wouldn't it take years to clean them out and replace them?

No. While you are at the Alpha level, program your subconscious mind for "Cancel! Cancel!". Send the instruction that whenever you hear someone putting themselves or you or anyone else down, you will say, "Cancel! Cancel!" and the thought or statement will be rejected. It will not become part of your experience.

But if I go around saying, "Cancel! Cancel!" all the time, people will think I'm nuts.

So say it silently to yourself. You do not have to flaunt it. Besides, if you are spending so much of your time around negativity, perhaps you might ask yourself why you are attracting negative energy to yourself. And by being a positive, happy, healthy person, you will find yourself attracting that kind of energy to you. You just watch!!

Keep in mind, you are responsible for the quality of your life. By achieving optimum mental health, that is, positive mental functioning, you will literally be making your dreams come true.

You say that Alpha is a great technique for detoxifying negative thoughts. How about using it directly for planting positive seeds?

Of course. You've heard of . . .

AFFIRMATION

Yes. That's telling yourself something over and over until you believe it. But why use Alpha? Why not just repeat positive statements?

You could. But remember, your subconscious mind carries out your instructions. And Alpha puts you in direct contact with your subconscious. Your conscious mind will argue with you. It is something like this:

> AFFIRMATION: Every day in every way I am getting better and better.

> CONSCIOUS MIND: Better than what? Who says so? In some ways you are getting worse.

> SUBCONSCIOUS MIND: You are getting better and better. Improve. Be the best you can be today. You are terrific!

or

> AFFIRMATION: You are in perfect health. Each day your health is improving.

> CONSCIOUS MIND: If you are in perfect health, how can it improve? You can't improve on perfection. And anyway, you are not perfect. Nobody is. What about that arthritis? How about that midriff I saw you with?

SUBCONSCIOUS MIND: Perfect health. Your body is healing itself. Your health is better than ever. Go, man, go!!

It pays to talk directly to your subconscious. It can see the possibilities and can help you become the best that you can be. And that is fantastic! Because you are fantastic!

I wish I were.

Cancel! Cancel! Grasp the possibilities and make them come true. Affirm your best self.

But what about problems? We all have them. I can't expect everything to go smoothly all the time. Be realistic.

Okay. Let's say you have a problem that you cannot seem to solve. What do you usually do about it?

I think it over. I worry about it. I hope it goes away.

Does the worrying help?

Not really.

How about trying another method? An excellent problem-solving technique is...

THE ALPHA SCREEN TECHNIQUE

Worrying about a problem gets you nowhere. Worry is like static on the radio; it interferes with your receiving the answers you seek. You can use your mind much more productively than that.

How?

The next time you have a problem to solve and you seem to be stuck, go to the Alpha level. Then mentally project your problem onto a screen. Surround that screen with a red haze.

Look at the problem from all angles. Examine all aspects of the problem in detail.

Hold it! You told me earlier that if I concentrate on a problem it will grow into a bigger problem. Caught you on that one.

That would be true if you simply left it at that. Your problem would get so big that even a huge theater screen would not be big enough. But that's the beauty of this technique. You are taking charge, rather than fretting about the problem. It's in the next step.

After you have looked at the problem and really explored it, change the haze around the screen from red to blue. The screen with the blue haze will be the solution.

Now concentrate on the solution. Look at it closely, in detail. See the problem solved. Enjoy the feeling of having solved the problem. Experience how good it feels not to have that problem weighing you down.

You mean if I do that, my problem will be solved? Just like that?

What this will do for you is set your subconscious mind on the road to solving it. Sometimes the solution will appear instantly. Other times it will take a while for the seed to germinate. But have faith in the power of your mind. The solutions to your problems lie within. You need only let your subconscious mind access those millions of billions of bits of information that are stored in your memory bank.

If I can use my mind to solve problems, I could also use it to attain my goals, couldn't I?

Certainly. Would you like a technique to help you attain your goals?

Of course!

Fine. This technique is called...

VISUALIZATION

I've heard of that. More and more people are talking about it. But I am not quite sure how it works.

Okay. First, let me remind you that what your mind can conceive and what you can believe, you can achieve. What are your personal goals?

I want to be rich!

That's kind of general. Be specific.

I want a million dollars, after taxes.

That's a start. Now, what is the first thing you will do when you get your million dollars?

If I get it.

Not if, when. You must believe it.

Okay. When I get my million dollars I will buy a house at the beach. I have always loved the seashore. I want a house there. I want to share it with my family and friends.

Fine. Write it down. Million dollars. House on the beach.

Now visualize yourself there, strolling with your

family on the shore. See the house. See the color, the shape. Look at the features. Visualize it in detail. See yourself in the house. See how it is furnished. Is there a fireplace? What type of furniture is there? What is the layout of the house?

Write these things down. Design your house at the beach.

Why write it down?

Writing goals down commits you to them. You are free to change them, of course. But writing down goals helps you focus on them. And when you visualize goals, you send electro-magnetic energy out. Your subconscious mind attracts to you what you expect to get.

Now that you have a goal and have written it down, you are ready for the key to visualization. You must **feel** it.

Feel it?

Yes. Actually imagine yourself already having attained the goal. Feel yourself enjoying the house at the beach. Hear the waves. See the seagulls. Feel the warm sand beneath your feet. Feel the glow of love coming from your family. However you really want it to be, write it down, visualize it, and feel it. Actually experience it.

The more you actually feel how it is to have attained

your goal, the closer that goal is to being realized in your life. More and more that goal is becoming part of your total experience.

You mean I can have anything if I use visualization?

The possibilities are endless! If you are willing to do what is necessary to attain your goals, you will achieve them.

Aha! I can't just visualize them. I have to do the work.

Of course. Look at it this way. You are working now. You are putting out energy and effort. But without clearly defined goals, you are probably going around in circles, not getting anywhere.

You are right there.

By having clearly defined goals, you can accomplish more with less effort than in the past. Goal setting and visualization work by focusing your energy. The same energy you expend now can be used to accomplish what you desire. That's much more productive than is aimless effort. And a whole lot less frustrating!

Opportunities will become available to you. You will see. And since you will be focused on your goals, you will be in a position to recognize them. Success is yours. Set goals, believe you will accomplish them. Achieve them.

Well, I haven't been that successful in the past. I might as well try it. I am not so sure I'm worthy of success, though. What did I do to deserve it?

Ah! That leads us into optimum emotional health.

CHAPTER FIVE

Achieving Optimum Emotional Health

You deserve the best of everything because you are terrific! You are brimming with talent and imagination. You deserve to fulfill your wonderful potential! And you deserve to enjoy this world to the fullest!

That's not what I was led to believe when I was growing up.

Then let me lead you to believe it now.

Do you want me to get a big head?

Yes.

You mean you want me to believe that I'm the greatest?

Yes.

Better than anyone else?

No. We are all the greatest. Each of us is the greatest. We all have the potential to be the best. It is simply a matter of...

SELF-ESTEEM

I love self-esteem. It feels good. It feels marvelous! I get such a warm feeling inside. I just swell up with well-being. I am at my emotional optimum level because I have self-esteem. And I feel that I deserve the best of everything. I am a real winner! I am fantastic!

Well, with an attitude like that, you must feel as though you are in a class by yourself. Doesn't it get lonely way up there?

Lonely? Not by a long shot. Boy! The better I feel about myself, the more I feel connected to the universe. I simply am doing my part, the best I can. And that's great.

I've always been taught to be modest. I can't stand conceited people.

I don't care for conceit either. Self-esteem is nicer.

Let me explain what I see as the difference between self-esteem and conceit. Self-esteem means feeling a sense of self worth. It is realizing that I have been blessed with some extraordinary gifts — love, talent, creativity, and more. Self-esteem helps me use those talents productively to achieve goals and to help humanity. I can't use them if I do not know I have them.

Conceit is different. Conceit means putting myself up there and others down there. A conceited person looks for faults in others in order to elevate himself. That's why people do not like conceited people. It is the conceited person who is the first to jump on a mistake or to say an unkind word.

And you know what? It is usually that conceited person who lacks self-esteem! If you find yourself tearing others down, it could be that you are trying to boost yourself up at their expense. Everyone loses that way. I prefer it when everybody wins.

But if you are spending time thinking you are great, where does that leave others? There's no time for them, is there?

Oh, yes there is. When I feel great, I feel a surge of love for others. The more I recognize my own best qualities, the more I look for the best qualities in others. So when I have self-esteem, I can better see that...

YOU ARE TERRIFIC!

How do you mean?

It is because I have self-esteem that I have a sense of well-being and happiness. When a person feels wonderful, he or she looks for the best in others. Winners want others to be winners too. No lose-lose situations. No win-lose situations. Only win-win situations. When I feel good about myself, I want to encourage the best in you. And you are terrific!

I wish you could convince me of that.

Nobody can convince you. You have to accept it for yourself. If you lack self-esteem, I could tell you how wonderful you are and you would not believe it. I could tell you a million wonderful things about yourself and each time you would come back with ten negative things. After awhile, you would probably say, "If you really knew me, you wouldn't say those nice things."

Yeah. I have actually thought that when I have been complimented.

You see, self-esteem is not a thinking thing. It is a feeling thing. It means self acceptance on a basic emotional level. It means feeling lovable, acceptable, worthy. It means feeling good inside, warm, loving. An honest compliment is an acknowledgement of your best self. Appreciate it.

Allow yourself to feel the warmth, the sense of well-being. Those are positive emotions. And . . .

POSITIVE EMOTIONS ARE HEALING

That warmth is actually healing energy surging through your body. Norman Cousins in **Anatomy Of An Illness** talked about the healing power of laughter. He actually gave his body a tool for healing itself.

Emotions actually set up a chemical reaction in the body. Positive emotions send healing energy throughout the body. When a person has a sense of well-being, he or she is literally being well.

Hugs are good for that. Next time you hug someone, allow yourself to feel the warm, healing power surge through your body. When people hug, they are helping themselves to health. They are triggering a positive chemical reaction in each other.

I'm not used to having a positive self concept. Where do I start?

Start by turning the corners of your mouth up. Raise your breastbone up about an inch. This throws your shoulders back and raises your head up, so you walk around like the winner you are! See the results, boy. Feel the results. You are on your way! You're wonderful! You are one of a kind. You are special!!

I feel kind of silly doing that.

That's because you are not used to it. Keep it up. You will see the wonderful difference. Your new attitude will bring positive results and those successes will bring more self-esteem. You will begin to blossom into the best you that you can be.

What about negative feelings?

Just as positive emotions heal. . .

NEGATIVE EMOTIONS ARE TOXIC

As I said, emotions set up a chemical reaction in your body. Negative emotions release poisons into the system. If you carry negative, hurtful feelings around, they lead to illness.

It definitely pays to achieve optimum emotional health. Not only does it feel good, but it actually helps the body keep itself at its optimum level. I would much rather feel good than bad, no doubt about it.

So would I. I wish it were as easy as just feeling good. There must be more to it than that, though.

Yes, there is. Often, negative feelings about oneself have been built up over many years. Some people go through their whole lives feeling hurt and resentful and terrible about themselves. They might have been told that they are stupid or clumsy or rotten or no good. They might have grown up with little or no self-esteem. It is not unusual. But it is unnecessary.

I certainly have some work to do on my emotional health. Where do I start?

You have already started by carrying yourself with confidence. Keep that up. And the next time you feel a negative, toxic emotion, ask yourself...

WHOM DO NEGATIVE EMOTIONS HURT?

The next time you get angry or feel resentful or disappointed; the next time you hate someone or something; the next time you feel any negative emotion, ask yourself where that pain is. Is the other person feeling that pain?

They might be hurting, too.

I'm not talking about how they are feeling. Let's stay with **your** feelings. You are responsible for your feelings. After all, they are your feelings, nobody else's. Think about it. Your negative, hurtful emotions are sending poisons throughout **your** body, not anyone else's.

I'll make 'em pay! I'll hurt them back. I'll get even! Then I will feel better. Revenge is sweet.

Oh? Then what happens when the other person comes back at you?

Then I really get into some serious revenge. I'm talking heavy revenge here.

Listen to yourself. The way you are going about it, you will end up with two seriously damaged people. Revenge might feel okay for an instant, but is it worth it? You are really hurting yourself as well as the other person. Do you want to do that to yourself? Aren't you worth more than that?

I guess so.

Come on now. You know so. You are a fine person. You deserve the best of everything. If you wanted to, you could use your fantastic imagination to think up ways to hurt people or to get back at them, but. . .

Yeah! First I'd wait until they were on their way to work. I'd rent a helicopter and fly over their car. Then I'd bounce up and down on the top of their car and scream insults at them. Boy!

Are you getting angrier just thinking about it?

Yeah! Yeah! Then I'd spread some vicious rumors about them. Get them fired. Maybe cause a divorce! Or worse, I'd, I'd. . .

Stop. That's enough. I get the point. You have a fine imagination.

Thanks. I'm just getting warmed up.

So is the other guy.

What?

Now there are two of you using your imaginations to destroy each other. You both lose that way. No matter how you slice it, you end up hurting. Next thing you know, you will have lost a friend.

So what? I never liked him anyway. Jerk!

Do you want to lose friends? Family members? Children? Spouse? Parents?

At least I won't have to be hurt anymore.

Sure you will.

Not if they are not around.

Yes you will. Every time you think about that person or hear his name or see his picture, those feelings will come up again, triggering the pain, the resentment, the hurt. Remember, you will be hurting yourself, nobody else. Aren't you worth more than that?

Smile. Bring those shoulders up. Walk with confidence. There! You are terrific. You deserve to feel terrific.

Yes. But how? When I am hurt, I'm hurt. I can't just switch it off like that!

Try. . .

USING ALPHA TO DETOXIFY YOUR EMOTIONS

Alpha again?

Yes, indeed! Marvelous tool, just marvelous. Here is a technique for emotional detoxification.

Just thinking about that guy drives me crazy!

How did it start?

This is going to sound silly. Promise you won't laugh.

I can't promise that. What happened?

Okay. I loaned him $10.00 and when I asked him for it, he denied I had loaned it to him...Hey, stop snickering!

Well, your friendships must be worth more than that to you. You are worth more than that.

That was just the start.

It could have ended there. And you can use Alpha to change it even now.

No I can't. What's done is done.

Not necessarily. While it is true that you cannot

change the past, you can change your present experience of the past.

Every time you think of something that happened in the past, you are bringing that past experience into the present. You are experiencing it again. As you said, every time you think of that person, that feeling of resentment returns.

Well, there's nothing I can do about that.

If that were true, you would be a prisoner of negative emotions. You would never be able to achieve optimum emotional health. You could never be happy. Fortunately, you can detoxify your negative emotions.

How?

By replaying your unhappy experiences. Here's how:

Go to the Alpha level. Now recall the original experience just as it happened up to the point when you felt the anger or resentment.

Now, here's the key. Change the ending. Imagine the experience just as you would have liked it to happen. Use your wonderful imagination here. Have the experience end very positively. And visualize how good it feels. Actually allow yourself to feel those positive, healing emotions.

When you have done that, you have erased the negative feeling and replaced it with a positive one. Now thoughts about that experience and that person will trigger healing energy. You will be practicing emotional detoxification. It is a great tool for emotional healing.

Does it really work?

Yes. It is miraculous. Not only does it give you a tool for detoxifying negative emotions, but it is a great aid to self-esteem. I'll give you an example from my own experience. Let's call it the case of...

PAPA'S REACTION

When I was a schoolgirl I was given an assignment to write an essay. I always enjoyed writing, and on this day I was in rare form. I put a lot into the essay and when I turned it in, I was confident.

When I got it back I was happy to see an A+ on it, with glowing comments from the teacher: "Outstanding! Shows great ability!" Needless to say, I was thrilled. Right after school I ran home to tell papa. Of course, most little girls want to please their fathers and I was no exception.

When I got home, I proudly showed him my essay. He looked at it, then at me. His only words were, "Where did you copy this from?"

I was devastated. I felt hurt and ashamed. My self-esteem was zero. I felt like a nobody. I could have walked under the belly of a snake with a tophat on.

That experience stuck in my mind, as traumatic experiences from childhood often do. Years later, my husband and I published a newspaper. I wrote a weekly column. Every week, when I sat down to write it, I could feel my father standing over my shoulder saying, "Where did you copy this from?" Each time that negative feeling returned. Until I learned this technique.

How did you replay it?

I played it just as it was, up to the point when I showed the essay to papa. I got it back with the A+ on it. I ran home excitedly. I handed the essay to papa. Then he looked at it and turned to me.

Then...

Papa took me in his arms and said, "Honey, this is brilliant! Boy! It looks professional. You have great talent." He went on and on for half an hour telling me how good it was and how terrific I was. When I fantasize, I do not mess around! As I told you, use your imagination here. Really get into it. The more positive, the better.

At this point in my replaying I could feel myself swell up with self-esteem. I felt on top of the world. Here was my papa giving me what everybody needs — love, acceptance, appreciation. It felt so good.

Now when I think about that experience I can feel the healing energy surging through me. Now when I have writing to do I feel papa standing over my shoulder saying, "You really have talent. You really can write. That's fine, just fine." It makes the world of difference for my self-esteem. And, believe me, with self-esteem...

YOU ARE A WINNER!

Self-esteem gives you confidence. And when you enter a situation with confidence, you are a winner. Winners set goals and achieve them. Winners succeed.

Winners know they deserve the best of everything. Winners want the best of everything for everybody. Winners see the best in themselves. Winners realize their potential. Winners help others realize their potential, too.

Winners live life to the fullest. Winners create win-win situations. Winners attract other winners.

You are a winner! You deserve the best of everything. You have talent and creativity. You walk with confidence. You set your goals high and you achieve them, time after time, because you are fantastic!

I'm working on it.

Good! If anything is blocking your success, if anything is preventing you from achieving optimum emotional health, if you are loaded down with negative, toxic emotions, take charge!

Whenever you find yourself feeling undeserving or unworthy or unhappy. . .

LET GO AND GO FORWARD

You want that beach house. Go for it. If you are feeling undeserving of it, it could be an early experience that keeps you down. Look at it. Go back to it. Replay it.

I know what it is. When I was a child we did have a house at the beach. But my father lost his money and we had to sell it.

And you wanted to be like your dad.

Yes. So I figured that if he couldn't keep that house at the beach, I would never get one. Or if I did, I would lose it too.

Change it. He lost his money and his beach house. That was his experience, not yours. You are in charge now. You want that million. You want that beach house. It's yours! Let go of that sad past; go forward to your bright future!!

Wow! I'm going to replay that whole experience. I am going to have it end my way, at the beach!

Terrific! I'll meet you there. We can stroll down the beach and talk about optimum spiritual health.

Addendum: An amazing incident occurred the other day. I had just concluded a class and was telling the students that this book was ready to go to the printer. As they rose to leave the classroom, I remarked to one of the ladies, "What a lovely blue dress, Mary Jo," and then blurted out, "I once had a dress just like it. I remember I was scheduled to enroll in high school in the fall, where girls were required to wear a middy and skirt. My mother bought me several outfits for the coming semester. However, we suddenly moved to the Hollywood High School district, where the clothes were not restricted and each girl outfashioned the other in the dresses they wore. My parents decided that since I had the uniforms, I would have to wear them! So there I was, the girl in the middy-skirt! Toward the end of the semester mother bought a remnant of blue dotted swiss material and hand-sewed a simple dress for me. . .rounded neck, sleeveless, skirt gathered at the hips. . .similar to the one Mary Jo was wearing. She let me wear it to school one day. The entire school (it seemed) noticed and came up to compliment me."

As I recalled and related the story, I choked up and burst into tears. Here I am, 74 years old, sobbing like a baby. The class was also teary, gathering around, hugging and comforting me!

This powerful, traumatic emotion after 60 years surfaced and erupted with the same intensity that I, as a teenager, must have felt, but had suppressed. The next year we moved back to San Diego, where the school I attended required the girls to wear middy-skirts. . .and I was "in step" again.

We are adding the incident to this book to illustrate the effect of emotional scars that are suppressed and fester and subliminally condition our lives!

In examining and analyzing this experience, it explains why I do not need to be "in fashion", but can wear or do whatever feels okay to me, rather than have to conform to the crowd.

Papa's, "Where did you copy this". . .my mother's forcing me to be different by dressing against the "in group," programmed me to be able to do **my** thing! (possibly over-compensating by flaunting my non-conformity). These were both very painful learning experiences, but I can now be grateful for both, realizing that they taught me to value being myself and appreciating the good in all situations!

CHAPTER SIX

Achieving Optimum Spiritual Health

You've seen how powerful your mind can be. Your subconscious mind, if productively directed, can bring abundance into your life. You are a success. You are a winner. Your goals are being achieved.

I have already achieved many of them. And the more I accomplish, the better I feel, which gives me the confidence and the enthusiasm to set and accomplish greater goals!

That's wonderful. You really are on your way. Shall we walk along the shore for awhile, just take in all of this beauty?

Don't have time. Got to run. Too busy. See you later.

Wait a minute. Take an hour out of your busy schedule.

What?! 60/1,440ths of my day? No way!!

You know, you have come a long way. When we first met, you were tired and sluggish. Now you're moving a mile a minute. That's great. How about taking a break? One hour, that's all.

Ten minutes.

Fifty.

Twenty, maximum.

Thirty.

That's a deal. Let's go...

...So what's so important that you have to drag me out here to the beach?

Drag you? You told me you love the beach — the shore, the warm sand, the surf, the creatures, the sunsets, all of that.

Yeah, yeah. Real nice. Now, what do you want to discuss?

I want to talk about...

A GREATER POWER

There is a force in the universe, a life force. It is an infinite power that you can tap into if you open yourself to it. It allows you to transcend yourself. It is what connects us. It gives meaning to our lives. Not just your life or my life, but all our lives, together.

You mean God.

Most people call it God. I do. Others call it nature, the superconscious mind, the power of the universe, the universal intelligence, the spiritual. If we are not in touch with it, we cannot be complete.

Why not?

Because the spiritual aspect of ourselves takes us out of our own private worlds and connects us with the universal. It is what gives us the sense of being part of a greater whole. It links us together as living beings.

So I'm just a cog in the wheel, a small, insignificant part of the universe. I'm like a speck of sand on this beach, is that it?

Here you've built me up, now you want to tear me down. Where is all this self-esteem you've been telling me about?

Self-esteem is wonderful. I want you to realize how great you are. Let's just put it into perspective.

How?

By achieving a balance. By developing a sense of humility.

Humility? How can I have self-esteem and humility at the same time? I'm either terrific or I'm not.

You can have both. In fact, humility enhances your self-esteem.

How?

Look around you and pick out a picture. Turn around and around until you have just the picture you want. Do you want the ocean, the sun, the sky, the clouds, the seagulls? How about those cliffs over there, with those neat caves? Or perhaps a shot of the houses along the shore? Do you want that couple walking over there to be in your picture? The fisherman? The ships? The dolphins? Or maybe you would like to make up a picture to include whatever you would like. You have the imagination. Get a picture in your mind, then snap the photograph.

Okay. I've got it.

Fine. Let's see it. Hey! That's a beautiful picture. Now

let's make a jigsaw puzzle out of it. We'll paste the picture onto some cardboard, then cut it into pieces. Then I will separate the pieces and mix them all up.

Fine.

Now, choose a piece.

I'll take that one. I like the colors, the shape. And it has part of the fisherman on it. I like surf fishing.

Okay. I'll take that piece of sky.

That piece is boring. There's nothing special about it.

Oh? I think it is just as special as your piece. They are both wonderful.

No way.

We'll see. Let's put this imaginary puzzle together. Except for one thing. I will hold my piece out.

The puzzle will not be complete.

That's right. And what you will notice when you look at the picture is the hole left by my missing piece. Your eye will not be drawn to your beautiful piece of the puzzle. It will be drawn to that empty space. That makes my piece just as important and special as yours. Without any one of the pieces, no matter how simple or plain, there is not a whole picture.

I see.

So you are one of many. And each of us is special. When I think of that, I get a sense of humility. But that does not take away from my self-esteem. In fact, it reminds me that...

WHAT YOU GIVE IS WHAT YOU GET, MULTIPLIED

Just as the last piece is put into place, something happens. It happens in an instant. Zap! You no longer have a bunch of pieces of a puzzle; you have a picture. And that picture is greater and more powerful and more beautiful than all the pieces.

The whole is greater than the sum of the parts.

Yes. And that's the secret to optimum spiritual health. The total beauty of the picture depends upon the contributions of all of the pieces, and in turn gives meaning to the parts.

Now let's give life to the puzzle. Imagine yourself as one of the pieces and the universe as the whole picture. Your contribution to the whole is multiplied by the contributions of each of the others. And all of our contributions are multiplied by the whole universe, which reflects back upon each of us.

To me, the spiritual side of life has to do with what I contribute to the universe. It is my moral code. It determines how I relate to others. If I relate in a loving, supportive way, I am helping to make the universe a more loving and supportive environment. We are all enhanced.

But not everyone thinks that way. What about those who lie, cheat and steal their way through life? If you are so lovey-dovey, they will take advantage of you, sure as shootin'.

I can't determine how anyone else will live. That is up to them. I am responsible for how I choose to live and how I relate to others.

As far as being taken advantage of, I don't believe in being a patsy. I am reasonably cautious. But I am not going to spend my life in fear. If I did, I would bring about that which I feared. I have better things to do.

I want to spend my time being the best person I can be. I want to optimize my physical, mental, emotional, and spiritual health. I am determined to be a healthy, happy human being who is doing my part to create a better universe. And anyway, I get a kick out of it.

What?

I get a kick out of contributing. It feels good. I like it.

But not everyone does.

That's up to them. I can only do what I feel is right. I can't judge anyone else. I am thankful for what I have, for my talents and abilities. I have a lot to offer the world. I am going to offer it.

That makes sense to me. In fact, I want to do something for you. What can I do?

You can get off my foot.

What?

My foot. You're standing on it.

Oh, sorry.

There. That's better. Thanks. We have a few minutes left. I would like to spend that time appreciating you.

Me?

Yes. You're terrrrrrrific! Without you in this world, I would be incomplete.

That goes both ways.

Yes...

TOGETHER WE STAND

I want the best for you. I want your life to be whole, complete. I want you to have optimum physical health, to feel your best at all times.

I want you to have optimum mental health, to think positive, life-affirming thoughts.

I want you to have optimum emotional health, to realize how terrific you are and that you deserve the best of everything.

And I want you to have optimum spiritual health, or be thankful for what you are, to share the wonderful talents, imagination and abilities that you have been blessed with, in order to help create a better universe for each of us.

I want you to enjoy life and the infinite abundance that the universe offers.

Thank you. I want the same for you.

Yes. Thank you. Together we stand. Together we win.

I would like to show you something now. It is a way of really feeling the healing power of the universe. Unfortunately, our thirty minutes are up.

Forget about that. Show me. I've got time.

Sorry. Don't have time. Got to run. Too busy. See you later.

Okay. Okay. I get the point. Now show me this secret of harnessing the healing power of the universe.

It's no secret. It's . . .

THE CIRCLE

Face your left palm up in front of you. Now face your right palm down, also in front of you. Put your right palm over your left palm facing each other without touching.

Now bring them closer together, but do not allow them to touch. If you look down, you will notice a circle created by your arms, which includes your body. It goes from your hands around through your heart and back to your hands.

Now take a deep breath and feel the energy flowing through you. You should be able to feel an actual energy between your palms.

I don't really feel it yet.

Fine. Pump your palms. Bring them closer together and farther apart, still without letting them touch. Can you feel the intensity grow as your palms get closer together and lessen as they separate?

Yes.

Now, that energy is the healing power of the universe, God's healing power, I believe, passing through you. It is helping to make you better and better, healthier and healthier, happier and happier. Remember, what you can conceive and believe, you can achieve. It is all there for you, for me, for each of us.

This feels good! I want to share it.

Good. May I join you?

Certainly.

Okay. Extend your left palm toward me and I will place my right palm over it, without touching. Extend your right palm toward me and I will place my left palm under it, without touching. Our vibrations are radiating toward each other.

Now we are sharing in that healing power. Together we are becoming better and better, healthier and healthier, happier and happier. Feel it. Share it.

Great! And we do not have to stop at the two of us, do we?

Oh, no. That's the beauty of the circle. It can be shared by anyone who chooses to join it. Left palm up, right palm down. Up and down, round and round.

I like that! It feels good! I feel the universe flowing through me. I feel humble and special at the same time.

Yes. You're terrific! And you deserve the best of everything.

Now let's walk back down the beach. I want to get back to the institute.

As we walk, would you mind if I ask you some questions? I would like to find out more about you and how you became aware of optimum health.

Fire away.

CHAPTER SEVEN

How I Got Into This

Here you are, 74 years old, and you are the full-time, active director of a health institute. You have so much energy and enthusiasm. I find that amazing. You look like you are in your fifties and you have the energy of a woman of twenty.

Well, actually I'm 18. But don't tell my grown sons.

I would almost believe it! You really are an example of optimum health. Tell me, how did you get into this? Have you always been health conscious?

No. Far from it. Many years ago I smoked cigarettes, drank alcohol and coffee, ate sugar, meat, dairy products — the whole deal. It wasn't until I was in my late thirties that I started to become aware of health issues. And from there it was a gradual process.

Was there anything in particular that sparked your interest?

Around 1950 a friend handed me a copy of **Prevention** magazine. It was my first real exposure to preventive health and the importance of nutrition.

You know, over the years you might be exposed to many influences, yet there are certain times when a particular book or magazine article or television program or lecture really hits you. That has happened many times in my life. When I am ready for something in my life, it makes a strong impression. That **Prevention** magazine was like that for me.

Were you ill? Did you have a life-threatening illness?

No. I was in average physical health, for someone who smoked, drank and ate less-than-optimum foods. But I was really impressed with that magazine, so impressed that I immediately gave up cigarettes and coffee. And as time went on, I eliminated refined foods, alcohol, meat, and other foods that are not supportive of optimum physical health. I gained a new respect for my body.

So you started with the physical.

Yes. At that time that's what people thought about when you mentioned health — the body, the physical. The thoughts, emotions and the spiritual were not seen as essential aspects of balanced health. Now, of course, there is more and more evidence that they are.

You mentioned that your own awareness came gradually. What was your next step?

It was another of those turning points that began a long process. It was a giant step to material achievement.

I happened to read **Think And Grow Rich** by Napoleon Hill. I was inspired by that book and by Claude Bristol's **Magic Of Believing**, Norman Vicent Peale's **Power Of Positive Thinking**, and Harold Sherman's **Know Your Own Mind.** These books convinced me that one should not have to scrounge for chicken feed, but one can expect and receive one's heart's desires from the abundant storehouse of the universe. If we think we can, we can! As Napoleon Hill said, "Anything the human mind can believe, the human mind can achieve."

And we did, in spades! In two short years my husband, Lew, and I went from a hand-to-mouth existence to a million dollars! Lew made the million in construction, building tract homes in the San Diego area. We attained what most people strive their whole lives for. We had wealth and social prominence. I had it all — the cars, the furs, the diamonds, everything. We were living in a beautiful home, right on the beach in Del Mar, just north of San Diego.

But then another significant event occurred. One day, in 1953, my life was changed forever. I recall it vividly.

It was storming outside. I could hear the wind, the surf, the torrential rains. I had a fire going in the fireplace, which I could see from my bedroom. I could have felt secure, happy, blessed, protected from the raging storm, but I didn't. I felt sad, unhappy, low.

As I stared at the fire, I thought about how I was feeling. I wondered why I was not happy. Here I had everything a person could ever want, yet I was not happy. **If I'm not happy now,** I thought, **I will never be happy.** And that thought depressed me more. **There has to be more to life than this,** I thought, as my sadness gave way to sleep.

As I slept, I dreamed. Now dreams, as you know, can be pretty mixed-up affairs. But this dream had a profound effect on me. In my dream, a man with a full, white beard, dressed in a flowing robe, came to me and put his hand on my shoulder. He said, "Raychel, remember the words of Plato: 'You have to crawl before you can walk.'"

Somehow that one statement seemed incredibly profound to me. I might have heard it a hundred different times from many different people in my life. But this time it really hit me. I guess when Plato talks, people listen.

I awoke with a real sense of enthusiasm. I had the feeling that this guy in my dream was going to protect me and that I was being told to go on a search — a search for the meaning of life or for direction in my life, something like that.

A few days later I was in a used-book store. I was coming up from the basement when I looked to my right and saw a book by Plato. I grabbed it, quickly paid for it, and rushed home. I had to find that quote.

And, sure enough, you found it.

No. It wasn't there. But the gist of what Plato was saying, at least as I read it, was that you have to search. You must learn step by step. You will not find happiness or contentment or purpose from outside yourself. Well, that made sense to me, since all of the trappings of success had certainly left a void inside of me.

What happened then? You said it was the beginning of a long process.

Not long after that, a friend of mine, Sally, introduced me to Arthur Norris, a professor who taught the great books program in the city schools. He was very well read in philosophy, the power of the mind, the emotions, and the spiritual aspects of life. He obviously came into my life at just the right moment. I was ready to open myself to these subjects, and I did.

We organized our own great books group. Every week, about twenty of us would meet, led by Arthur. We would have lively discussions about various books that we had been assigned. The discussions were especially exciting when the topics were controversial, such as politics and philosophy. But my special interest was in the power of the mind.

So that's where you learned about the importance of a positive mental attitude and about visualization.

Arthur was my mentor in terms of mental and emotional issues and how they relate to a general sense of well-being. But the actual technique of visualization is a different story. I learned about that in a most fascinating way.

I attended a lecture one night in 1957. The lecturer told us that we could have anything we wanted if we used visualization. If we wanted a Cadillac, fine. Whatever we wanted, we could use visualization to get it.

Well, I didn't want a Cadillac, but I did want a T-Bird. I was wearing a salmon colored dress that night, so I thought I'd like that color. I felt myself in the car, driving around town. People were turning their heads and staring as I passed. I do not do things half way, so in my visualization I was the hit of the show.

I'll bet!

After the lecture, I put it out of my mind until a few

days later. Lew came home one evening and asked if I wanted a T-Bird. Now I knew that I had not said anything to him about my visualization, so I was surprised. I asked him what color it was, but he didn't know.

But when he brought it home, it was salmon colored.

Yes. Just as I had visualized it. The story I got was that a local car dealer had been given an allotment of three T-Birds and this one had been ordered by Don Ameche. But the dealer thought that it would be good for his business to sell it to a local person, someone who would be seen around town in the car. Three or four days after I visualized the car, he ran into Lew on the golf course and thought of me.

That could have been a coincidence.

I suppose one could see it that way. But I don't. The more I became aware of the power of the mind, the less I believed in coincidence. And over the years, the results have borne me out.

So you started visualizing more and more cars and furs and diamonds, and unlimited wealth.

No. The T-Bird was just a whim. But it did reinforce what I was learning in books. I am a person who believes in results, and that was a tangible result. I had already

137

realized that those things were not bringing me happiness or a sense of well-being. They were really part of my husband's dream, not mine.

I remember Lew saying that he didn't care if he was a millionnaire. He just wanted to live like one. And we did for a few years. Then with poor judgment and bad investments he lost his fortune. He spent the rest of his life trying to pay back debts.

That's awful!

Yes. It was devastating. Not only did his self-esteem suffer, but so did his physical health. He died in 1967. The official cause of death was heart failure. To me, though, Lew died of a broken spirit. And you know something, I truly believe that had he been aware of a program like the one at the Institute, he would be alive today. I believe that with my whole being.

Is that why you started the Institute? As a tribute to Lew?

His death was certainly a major influence, but there were others. Learning about Alpha was one of the most important.

How did that happen?

When Lew died, I developed a serious respiratory

condition. I had suffered from respiratory problems off and on since childhood, but after Lew's death they got worse.

I went to a doctor who diagnosed my condition as bronchial asthma. He began treating me with medication, but after several months I was not improving. When I asked him what he could do, he told me that there was nothing that could be done. I would never improve. The best I could hope for was that it would not get worse, and even that was a long shot. Well, I wasn't about to take that. I knew that if I stayed with that one, I'd be a goner in no time.

One day in 1970 I saw an ad in the newspaper which read something like, "Achieve health, wealth, and success. Learn to harness the power of your mind." What caught my eye was the word "health." The ad announced a lecture on Silva Mind Control. I went.

As it turned out, the lecture was about Alpha and how to use it. Over the years, I had learned a great deal about mental functioning, positive mental attitude, and visualization, but I was impressed by the practical approach that the speaker took. Here was a way for me to put my learning to practical use.

At the end of the lecture the speaker announced a course that would be starting the next night. I took the course and was impressed with it. It was practical; it was useful; it was a positive approach. But more than that, it showed me, for the first time, the connection between our thoughts and the rest of our being. Things began to fall into place. My symptoms diminished for the first time in three years. I had gotten a new lease on life. I was sold.

When the course was over, I continued with Alpha. I took advanced courses and became a certified instructor in Alpha Dynamics.

Your friends must have been impressed.

Impressed? Are you kidding? Most of them thought I had gone off the deep end. They really thought that this gal had flipped! They thought I was into some kind of mumbo-jumbo or something. Only Sally, the friend who introduced me to Arthur Norris, remained on friendly terms with me. She is still my best friend.

Most of the others took off in a hurry. Once a week for 20 years I had played cards with a group of women. When they found out that I was teaching mind control, they disbanded the group and re-formed it without me.

That must have been quite a blow. Did you stay with your teaching anyway?

Yes. I saw such wonderful results and I found I had no time for socializing, so I went on teaching Alpha and taught it until 1976. Then another of those critical events happened, something that would lead me to open the Institute.

At the end of March, 1976, I learned that a dear friend of mine, Thelma, had cancer. It was a total shock to me. She seemed to have everything going for her. She had initiated and developed a successful international communications enterprise. She was beautiful and warm. She was a pleasure to know. And here she had gotten cancer! That, in itself, was devastating. But I had lost two sisters to cancer, too. It seemed as though we were facing an epidemic.

That day I resolved to do something about it. I did not know what I could do, but I knew that the answer would be revealed to me somehow. And it was, very soon.

I prayed, asking for guidance. And I decided to go on a fast for as long as it would take me to find my mission. I fasted on water only for 18 days. On the 19th day my prayers were answered. I was told of a lecture by Eydie Mae Hunsberger, who had written **How I Conquered Cancer Naturally.** I had not heard of Eydie Mae, but the title of the book sent shivers up my spine.

I ran out and bought a copy of the book. I was up half the night reading it. I could not put it down. In the book, Eydie Mae told of how she had been diagnosed with terminal cancer, had gone to Ann Wigmore's Hippocrates

Health Institute in Boston, and had beaten cancer by adhering to the program.

Halfway through the book I said, "that's it!" In a flash I knew what I was going to do in the next phase of my life. I was going to open Hippocrates West in the San Diego area. I did not know how I was going to do it. But I did know it would happen and I knew it would be soon. I was inspired and I was determined.

I went to the lecture and was further inspired by Eydie Mae. Here was a dynamic and enthusiastic woman who had, six years earlier, been given only a few months to live.

After her lecture I went up to her and told her that I was going to open an Hippocrates Institute in San Diego. She said, "That's nice," but I could tell she did not really believe me. She did tell me, though, that Dr. Ann Wigmore was going to be in San Diego in a couple of weeks.

The ball was really rolling now! I went to Ann Wigmore's lecture. I arrived early, but even then Dr. Ann was surrounded by people. There was no way I could get near her. I asked someone to deliver a note to her. On the note I had written, "It is imperative that I see you."

Dr. Ann must have thought that I was seriously ill or something, because she left the crowd and came over to me. I introduced myself and told her that I had decided to open Hippocrates West in San Diego.

She patted me on the shoulder and said, "That's nice, dear," and started to walk away. I put my hand on her arm and said, "No, I'm serious. I am going to do it." Again she said, "That's nice," and started to walk off. But I persisted. I was almost hanging on her, trying to get her to take me seriously.

You certainly had your nerve!

You bet! I felt this was my mission. I was not going to let anything dissuade me. I was determined! I guess Dr. Ann finally saw that I was really serious, so she suggested that I start by going through the program in Boston.

I made a reservation for three weeks starting on May 30, 1976. From that point on things started falling exactly into place. While I was waiting to go to Boston, I located a place in El Cajon, east of San Diego. It was a three bedroom, two bath cottage set beautifully on a 12½ acre avocado grove. It seemed the perfect place for the Institute.

I called the owner to inquire about it, but he informed me that he had just leased it out for two years. I could not believe it, because it seemed so right. And, sure enough, a few days later the owner called me back to inform me that the people who had leased the property had been transferred and that it was available again. I told him that I would check out the program in Boston and if it was what I had been led to believe it was, I would call him.

The program obviously lived up to your expectations.

Oh, yes. It was amazing. I was sold. People with a variety of dis-eases were reporting dramatic changes. As far as the physical aspects of health, this was the absolute optimum program. I was more determined than ever that Hippocrates West was to become a reality.

I phoned the landowner from Boston to tell him that I wanted the property. He told me that there were two parties who were very interested in it. They were virtually fighting over it. I told him that I was still interested and that I would call him when I got back to San Diego. Somehow I knew that if that was the right place for the Institute, nothing could stop it. And I had a strong feeling that it was.

When I returned to San Diego I called him. He told me that he could not figure out how it happened, but the two parties who had been so determined to lease the property a couple of weeks earlier had somehow mysteriously lost interest. Not one, but both at the same time. He could not believe it!

I could. It was a miracle. And I believe in miracles. I signed the lease. We opened on September 19, 1976.

Was it a struggle in the beginning or did it take off immediately?

Right from the beginning it was a success. Before we opened, I had a showing of the site. I had put fliers in all of the health food stores around San Diego. Hundreds of people showed up. Someone asked me when we were going to open and without thinking, and before I could stop myself, I told her we would be open in three weeks.

How did you expect to organize a health institute in such a short time?

I didn't. As I said, it just came out. How it was going to get done was a mystery. But we did open three weeks later. People came from all over to help get that place ready. All of the work was volunteer labor. People came to paint, to fix things up, to lend a loving hand. It was marvelous.

On the day we opened I was leaving the property to go to my place in San Diego to get dressed and I noticed that the building was an awful color. I mentioned to someone that a nice pale yellow would be better. By the time I returned, the front of the building had been painted. The 14 guests who were checking in and others who were around, had chipped in to do it. It has always been like that at the Institute. People working together, giving of themselves to create a place of love and beauty.

So you started with 14 guests.

Yes. And very quickly the numbers grew. In fact, within two months we had outgrown that location. We had to put guests up in apartments and motels in the area. We began looking for another site right away. It took us two years to find our present location in Lemon Grove, just east of downtown San Diego.

Since we opened in 1976, many thousands of people have been through the program. It has evolved into the Optimum Health Institute of San Diego.

What changes have you made over the years?

As far as the nutritional and detoxification aspects of the program, I have kept it pure, just as it was when I went through the program ten years ago. I still believe it is the optimum program for detoxification and nourishment. And I have seen such amazing results over the years that I am as convinced as ever.

The only changes I have made have resulted from my own experience and learning over the past thirty-five years. As I have said, I truly believe that in order to achieve optimum health, one cannot neglect any part of one's being — the physical, the mental, the emotional, the spiritual. Each is essential.

Well, that's it. That is how I got to the here and now from the there and then.

So for you it has been a thirty-five year journey.

Yes. An exciting one. And I am just beginning. I have so much more living to do, so many more fascinating adventures, so many delightful challenges!

You certainly are an inspiration! And you've given me a great deal to think about.

Think it over. Learn as much as you can about optimum health. Master the techniques I have shared with you. Give it a try. And please keep in touch. I would love to hear from you.

I will. One last thing before we part, Raychel.

Yes?

How about a hug?

You've got it, kiddo!!

Ooooooooooooooooooooo. . .eeeeeeeeeee! That feels great!!

EPILOGUE

Hi, Raychel. Remember me?

Of course. We shared a cloud about a year ago.

We certainly did. And since then I have turned my entire life around. I am a whole new person, inside and out!

I'll say! You've become that fantastic person I recognized in you from the start.

I'm so glad you did. It was the turning point in my life. I will admit I was skeptical at first. When we parted, I was not so sure about this optimum health stuff. But you convinced me enough to at least try it. Do you know what did it?

What?

You. I thought about this 74-year-old woman, so full of energy and life! At age 63, when most people are thinking of retiring and just existing until they die, you started a whole new career. And to hear you tell it, you are always looking for new, exciting challenges. I was inspired! So I decided to give it a try.

Excellent.

And you know something, it works! It really works!! In three weeks I dropped a notch on my belt and I have leveled off at three notches. I am at my ideal weight and I have more energy than I ever thought possible.

It shows!

Thanks. I never realized how important thoughts are. I used to tell myself I was fat, sluggish, low energy. Rather than look at the possibilities, I was stuck on that image. And no matter how many times I would lose weight or start an exercise program, I could never keep to it. But this time was different. I finally looked down at my toxic waist and said, "That's it, fella! You go, permanently!!"

The hardest part, where my weight was concerned, was when my friends would say things such as, "You've been on so many diets. You will lose the weight, then gain it right back, plus a few pounds."

Whenever I heard that, I would say to myself, "Cancel! Cancel! You are not fat. You are trim, energetic, well toned. Your body is a showpiece!"

The pounds just melted off. And with success in that area I gained confidence. I was no longer willing to lead a mediocre existence, just getting by day to day. Not me, boy! I was, and am, determined to make of myself the best piece of the puzzle I can be.

You've got the picture! And what a beautiful picture it is with you in it. I am proud of you. There is such a vibrant glow about you. You actually sparkle.

That's coming from inside. My life used to be fraught with problems. Things just did not seem to go my way. I was quick to anger. My relationships suffered and I was unhappy.

Now, instead of problems, I have challenges. While I am still confronted by snags along the road of life, I meet my challenges with enthusiasm and a positive attitude. My goals are more sharply defined than ever before and I am achieving them. When I am in a situation that used to anger me, I simply use the three-finger technique, calm myself and approach the situation in a positive, constructive, life-affirming manner. No longer do I allow disagreements to escalate into life or death battles. I feel great! And for the first time I am in control of my life.

I knew you could do it. And I am so glad you did.

I am too, Raychel. Thanks. And you know the best part?

What's that?

Look at my left hand.

A wedding band! Well!! Where's your bride?

Oh, she is out looking at houses.

At the beach?

At the beach!

You mean you already have your million?

I'm working on it. And I will achieve it!

You know something, kiddo? You've got it all. Optimum health...and a new bride, too!

You really are terrrrrrific!!

RECIPES

Many people have grown up believing that if a food is good for you, it has to taste awful. I don't believe that. Raw foods, properly combined, are nutritious and delicious. Once you get the hang of combining raw foods, I am sure you will agree!

I have included a few of my favorite recipes to get you started. Note that many of the recipes call for Quick Sip. What I am referring to is Dr. Jensen's Quick Sip. It is made without salt or sugar and can be used in any recipe calling for salt or seasonings. It is available in most health food stores. I suggest you use it sparingly; a few drops go a long way.

Sample these recipes, then use your own wonderful imagination to create your own masterpieces!

REJUVELAC

1 part soft spring wheat berries
3 parts purified water

Wash and strain the wheat berries. Put them into a container. Add purified water. Cover with a screened lid. Soak for 24 hours. Pour the water into a jar. That soak water is rejuvelac. To make more, use the same wheat berries and add more water. You can do this twice before changing the wheat berries. You can drink rejuvelac straight or use it in other recipes.

SEED SAUCE

⅔ cup sprouted sunflower seeds
⅓ cup sprouted sesame seeds
½ cup rejuvelac

Blend sesame seeds with ¼ cup rejuvelac. When creamy, add sunflower seeds and remaining ¼ cup rejuvelac. Blend again until creamy. Pour into a bowl. Leave at room temperature overnight. Drain off and discard liquid. Cover and refrigerate seed mixture until needed. It will keep for a couple of days. Before serving, add more rejuvelac, if desired, to achieve desired consistency. Serve over sprouts, vegetables and greens.

SAUERKRAUT

3 large heads grated cabbage (outer leaves reserved)
2 Tbs. ground kelp (available in health food stores)
2 tsp. garlic (optional)
2 tsp. ground caraway (optional)

Grate cabbage. Put into one-gallon or larger crock or jar. Add seasoning. Cover with reserved outer leaves of cabbage. Place large plate and a weight on top. Leave at room temperature for five days. Remove scum and leaves, and mix so juice is evenly distributed. Place in refrigerator, covered. It will keep for weeks.

AVOCADO SAUCE

2 ripe tomatoes
2 avocados
2 green onions
Pinch dill weed
Pinch oregano and/or basil
Quick Sip to taste
Rejuvelac for consistency
2 tsp. lemon juice

Blend first three ingredients. Add other ingredients and blend thoroughly. Serve over sprouts, greens, or vegetables.

VEGETABLE SAUCES

2 or 3 vegetables of your choice
Rejuvelac for desired consistency
2 Tbs. sauerkraut or ½ tsp. Quick Sip
2 green onions
Pinch oregano, cumin, or other flavoring

Blend vegetables, sauerkraut and rejuvelac. Add flavorings and blend again. Serve over sprouts, greens, or vegetables.

GUACAMOLE

3 medium avocados, diced or mashed
1 small yellow onion, finely chopped
2 medium tomatoes, diced
Pinch oregano
Pinch basil
Quick Sip to taste
Juice of ½ lemon

Mix avocado and onion lightly. Add oregano, basil, quick sip and lemon juice. Mix again, lightly. Spread tomatoes over top and refrigerate. Mix tomatoes in just before serving.

FARMER'S CHOP SUEY

3 green onions, thinly sliced
2 tomatoes, finely diced
1 tsp. ground dill weed
1 cup seed sauce·
Quick Sip to taste
4 or 5 cucumbers, diced
1 bunch radishes, thinly sliced
1 bell pepper, finely chopped

Mix first 5 ingredients and allow to marinate for one hour. Add last three ingredients and serve. For variation, make broccoli delight by adding 1 lb. chopped broccoli to Farmer's Chop Suey. Or you can make cauliflower supreme by adding one head chopped cauliflower instead of broccoli.

COLESLAW

1 large cabbage, finely shredded
Several radishes, sliced
Several scallions, sliced
2 tomatoes, finely diced
2 carrots, shredded
½ cup seed sauce
1 Tbs. ground caraway or dill
Quick Sip to taste

Mix all ingredients and serve.

VEGETABLE LOAF

1 cup shredded carrot
1 large bunch celery, finely chopped
1 bunch green onions, finely chopped
2 green peppers, finely chopped
½ bunch parsley, finely chopped
2 zucchini, shredded
½ cup ground sunflower seeds
1 Tbs. basil
⅓ cup ground sesame seeds
Pinch of your favorite spice
Quick Sip to taste

Mix ingredients. Strain. Knead well. Place in a dish or pan. Place in food dehydrator or cover with glass and place in sunny spot for 6 hours. Serve as a main course. For variety, form into balls instead of loaf before dehydrating.

MARINATED MUSHROOM SALAD

1 lb. mushrooms, sliced or chopped
2½ cups sauerkraut, liquified
1 medium onion, finely chopped
Quick Sip to taste

Combine ingredients in bowl and marinate overnight in refrigerator. Add, as desired, raw peas, diced green peppers, tomatoes, zucchini, or yellow summer squash.

FRUIT SOUP

6-8 apples, peeled and cored
1 cup rejuvelac

Blend apples with rejuvelac. To vary, add any sweet or sub-acid fruit (pears, peaches, sweet plums, bananas, grapes). These can be blended with apples or diced and added when serving.

GAZPACHO

4 medium tomatoes
2 Tbs. sauerkraut
2 cucumbers, finely diced
½ bell pepper, finely diced
2 green onions, thinly sliced
Pinch basil or dill weed

Blend 2 tomatoes and the sauerkraut. Dice remaining two tomatoes and add, along with remaining ingredients. Serve.

ACKNOWLEDGMENTS

I gratefully acknowledge my appreciation to the many hundreds of dear persons who, through the past decade, have suggested what seemed like an impossible feat, "You must write a book to share your experiences and the metamorphoses you have witnessed at the Institute."

To the thousands whose lives have touched mine in nearly three-quarters of a century — inspiring, encouraging, criticizing, praising, supporting and loving me.

To my wonderful departed husband of 36 years, Lew, who encouraged me to dream and to follow my dreams. To our progeny: Three sons, five grandsons, a granddaughter and four great granddaughters, all precious to me.

To my adopted children — the many thousands of students who have attended the Institute — who are also very special to me, and without whose attendance I could not be celebrating the tenth anniversary as founder and director of the Optimum Health Institute of San Diego.

A special acknowledgment to Sally Schissell, who pointed me toward this path 35 years ago; Anthony A. Calabrese, who coined the title COMING ALIVE; Sam and Afton Dunbarr, who walked into my life one auspicious day seven years ago and offered their time, energy, and talents to the Institute.

And, of course, to Eydie Mae and Arn Hunsberger, and Pam and Bob Nees, who have been by my side from the beginning, my deepest gratitude.

Here's to life, yours and mine! Long may it continue to improve, bringing Heaven on Earth to each generation!!

With love,

Raychel